ST. M   A

ST. MONICA

The Power of a Mother's Love

Giovanni Falbo

Pauline
BOOKS & MEDIA
Boston

Library of Congress Cataloging-in-Publication Data

Falbo, Giovanni.
  [Santa Monica. English]
  St. Monica : the power of a mother's love / Giovanni Falbo. — 1st English ed.
    p. cm.
  Translated by Matthew Sherry.
  Includes bibliographical references.
  ISBN 0-8198-7099-4 (pbk.)
  1. Monica, Saint, d. 387. 2. Augustine, Saint, Bishop of Hippo. I. Title. II. Title: Saint
Monica.
  BR1710.F3213 2007
  270.2092'2—dc22
  [B]

                               2006033352

Cover design by Rosana Usselmann

Cover art: Ary Scheffer (1795–1858), *St. Augustine and His Mother St. Monica,* Louvre, Paris, France. Photo credit: Rèunion des Musées Nationaux / Art Resource, NY.

Interior photos by Mirella Sciattella

"P" and PAULINE are registered trademarks of the Daughters of St. Paul.

Original edition published in Italian under the title Santa Monica

Copyright © 2003 Edizioni San Paolo, s.r.l. – Cinisello Balsamo (MI)

Translated by Matthew Sherry

First English edition, 2007

Published by Pauline Books & Media, 50 Saint Paul's Avenue, Boston, MA 02130-3491. www.pauline.org.

Printed in the U.S.A.

Pauline Books & Media is the publishing house of the Daughters of St. Paul, an international congregation of women religious serving the Church with the communications media.

1 2 3 4 5 6 7 8 9   11 10 09 08 07

Contents

Introduction

For some time now I have wanted to write a book on the life of St. Monica. I've searched St. Augustine's writings for the historical and literary material necessary for such a book. My desire was reinforced by continual requests from people who wanted to know more about Monica. I situated her life in the environment and culture of her time, the fourth century, which is my specialty as a scholar. During my research on existing biographies, I discovered insufficiencies and mistakes that I tried to correct, although I realized that this was too ambitious a plan, and that I would inevitably make some mistakes myself.

The majority of references to St. Monica's life are found in the works of St. Augustine, especially in his *Confessions.* Up until Book Nine of that work, and especially in Book Nine, Augustine's life is completely interwoven with his mother's. In *The Dialogues of Cassiciacum,* and particularly in the works *On the Blessed Life* and *On Order,* St. Monica is a participant in the dialogues. Her responses form an outline of her character.

Clues about her can also be found in many of Augustine's other works, and I will mention these where appropriate.

One has a definite sense of humility before the writings of Augustine; a reverential fear before such a great thinker and artist. For this reason, many authors have not wanted to waste Augustine's words and have composed brief biographies of St. Monica by assembling a number of selections from the writings of her son. The result is like a splendid necklace formed of many pearls. Fr. N. Concetti took this approach in his book *Volgarizzazione della vita di S. Monica scritta da S. Agostino* (A Translation of the Life of St. Monica as Written by St. Augustine, Rome, 1919). Closer to our own time, Augustinian Fr. A. Eramo gathered together in his book *Mia madre Monica* (Edizioni Gioia, Rome, 1974) the most important passages regarding Monica from the work of St. Augustine. Above all, the famously talented scholar Fr. Agostino Trapè used this approach in his book *Sant'Agostino: Mia madre* (Edizioni Ancora, Milan, 1975).* In this work, he added a substantial introduction and a well-documented outline of the life of St. Monica to a wide selection of texts taken from St. Augustine.

Although I have great respect for such works, I saw the need for a genuine biography written with a bit of stylistic freedom. All biographies begin from their sources, but a mere list of facts copied from these sources, as complete as that may be, is not enough.

In the nineteenth century, French Bishop Emile Bougaud wrote an extensive biography entitled *Histoire de Ste. Monique* (Paris, 1865), which was produced in a number of editions and translations, including English. The biography begins from the

---

*This book, translated into English by Matthew O'Connell and titled *My Mother* (Augustinian Press, 1987), is currently not in print. —Ed.

Augustinian texts, and the famous author demonstrates his extensive knowledge of these. But in my opinion, the book contains a number of defects that make it impossible to recommend in its present form to readers today. Bishop Bougaud was a respected scholar of the lives of the saints, but the period he specialized in was the seventeenth century (as he demonstrated in his life of St. Francis de Sales). When it comes to the period in which St. Monica lived, the fourth century, gaps appear in his knowledge. This is evident in the imprecise historical information that Bishop Bougaud provides when he sets aside Augustine's writings in order to place the facts within their context: many of his dates and sequences of events are inexact. Moreover, without critical scrutiny he accepts, together with the writings of Augustine, the traditions related in the breviaries of the Hermits of St. Augustine. A reader unfamiliar with this material may not realize how much of it is truly historical and how much is legend. One further observation I have is that, since the source material is lacking, Bishop Bougaud tends to stretch it out with unnecessary annotations, repetitions, and rather wild conjectures. The result is a book that makes for tiresome reading.

The purpose of this new biography of St. Monica is to provide a succinct but thorough description of her life, beginning of course with the writings of St. Augustine. These will be situated within their historical context in an effort to bring to life the human and Christian character of the saint.

I hope that this book will both encourage those who read it to imitate what they find here and reward those who asked that it be written.

CHAPTER I

Tagaste in Numidia

St. Monica[1] was born at Tagaste, in Numidia, in 331.[2] Numidia, an ancient Berber kingdom once located in North Africa, corresponds today to the eastern part of modern Algeria. It is a sweltering land. Few may recall ancient history lessons about the Numidians' fierce struggle against Rome, which finally subjected them to its Empire. Rome, however, was not able to change this people's view of life or completely absorb them into its own civilization. Monica belonged to the Numidian people, volatile and headstrong, who had opposed Rome together with their king, Jugurtha, wearing down the resistance of generals like Albinus, Metullus, and the famous Marius.

By the time of St. Monica's birth, centuries after these events, the Roman Empire had introduced its customs, laws, and language everywhere. Despite this, the Numidians did not lose their awareness of being a unique people. The historian Procopius,[3] who wrote during the sixth century, shows that in his day the Punic language was still being spoken by part of the population of northwestern Africa.

Roman culture was enriched by contributions from the African spirit; we think of Terence, a playwright who was born in Carthage, and Apuleius, author of *The Golden Ass,* who came from Madaurus, the town near Tagaste where Monica sent Augustine for his secondary studies.

Particularly relevant is the expansion of the Christian community that made Numidia a land of saints and prepared the way for Monica's development. Monica grew up in an atmosphere that had seen the fervor of the first generations of Christians in Africa, who with their blood spilled during the persecutions both sowed and watered the seeds of Christianity.

One of the most reliable documents on the first-century martyrs is the account of the first Numidian martyrs, compiled by the Roman proconsul. These witnesses from the tiny city of Scillium—three men: Speratus, Nartzalus, and Cintinus; and three women: Donata, Secunda, and Vestia—were examined by the proconsul, Vigellius Saturninus, who resided in Carthage. One interesting detail from their interrogation concerns the treasure that they guarded jealously: they had a case containing scrolls of the New Testament, which were briefly described, providing a glimpse of the early canon of Scripture. This example predates the *Muratorian Fragment*★ by a few years. The martyrs displayed their Numidian spirit in their combination of simplicity and unshakable determination; after courageously professing their faith and refusing to sacrifice to the gods, they were decapitated. It was July 17 of the year 180.

Prior to this date, no reliable information exists about the Church in this proconsular African province,[4] except for the

---

★ A copy of the oldest known listing of canonical books. —Ed.

archaeological evidence of the catacombs of Adrumetum, the capital of Byzacena. In the martyrs of Scillium, therefore, we honor the origin and roots of the luxuriant tree that bore so many fruits of holiness in Africa. There is evidence of other martyrs during the reign of Emperor Commodus (180–192), in the letters that the pagan orator Maximus of Madaura sent to St. Augustine. These are martyrs who bear Punic names: Mygdon, Samae, Namphanio, and Lucitas. Nothing more is said of them, except for Maximus's wonder and incomprehension that one could renounce the splendid and illustrious Greek divinities in the name of someone who had ended his life on such a shameful instrument of death as the cross.

Toward the end of the second century this land gave birth to the genius of Tertullian. He expressed the profound and demanding message of Christ in the Roman tongue for the first time, and in such a way that he is considered the founder of ecclesiastical Latin. Tertullian, too, had a fiery African temperament, as demonstrated by his gift for scorching criticism and his ability to pummel his opponent with a flow of speech as swift as a rushing tide. After him, Africa boasts the great St. Cyprian, a converted orator who became the bishop of Carthage toward the middle of the third century. He not only dominated the scene in the Church in Africa, but in the universal Church as well, through his pastoral leadership, his letters, and his tracts illustrating the persecutions of Decius (250–251) and Valerian (257–258). It was during the latter of these that Cyprian too gave the ultimate witness of shedding his blood in the name of Christ.

These famous names are just the tip of the iceberg. They point to the nameless throngs of heroic Christians who stand behind them. Tertullian, in fact, wrote of the "thousands of Christians who exposed themselves to the blows of persecution" during the reign of Septimus Severus (202–203). We have an authentic account of the martyrdom of Perpetua and Felicity that took place during this persecution and may even have been compiled by Tertullian. With contagious enthusiasm, he wrote in his *Apology:* "We are but of yesterday, and we have filled every place among you—cities, islands, fortresses, towns, marketplaces, the very camp, tribes, companies, palace, senate, forum...."[5] In a word, Christianity had set down roots in every social class. Africa's ecclesiastical hierarchy was also firmly established, as can be seen by the first regional Council of Carthage, which was held during the early 200s and gathered seventy bishops from Proconsular Africa and Numidia under the presidency of Agrippinus.[6] Roughly thirty years later, the Council, led by Donatus, gathered ninety bishops together; and about the same number, many of them from Numidia and Mauritania, met for the Council headed by Cyprian in 256.

The great number of apostates during the persecution of Decius and the great number of martyrs during that of Valerian also indicate the widespread distribution of Christianity throughout Africa during the century before Monica lived.

Half a century later, after the long period of peace during which the Church in Africa made still further progress, more fiery apologists of the Christian faith appeared, all of them converts from paganism. There was Arnobius, a native of Sicca in Numidia, who after a dream changed from a persecutor of Christianity into one of its defenders. He composed a seven-part apologetic work against the pagans. Lactantius, a contemporary of Arnobius, was the author of works on creation and of the *Divine Institutes;* he reached the height of his expressive and stylistic powers with the book, *On the Manner in Which the Persecutors Died.*

The peace Constantine established after the last bloody persecution from 303 to 311, which had claimed a great number of martyrs throughout the Empire during those eight long years, was nothing more than a civil peace for Africa. Years of persecution had also seen the dangerous growth of the Donatist schism, which divided African Christianity for more than a century. This schism essentially began out of ambition and personal hostility toward Mensurius, the bishop of Carthage. Then doctrinal factors came into play: the ordination of Mensurius's successor, Caecilian, was challenged on the pretext that the consecrating bishops had been unworthy. The proponents of the schism elected Majorinus as bishop and deposed Caecilian, who soon became bishop of Casae Nigrae in Numidia and head of the Donatist sect there. The heart of the Donatist heresy was the mistaken idea that the sacraments were valid only if the minister conferring them was holy. If such an idea were true, the obvious result would be that one would never be able to know if the sacraments were validly celebrated. This undermined the very foundation of the Church, as there would no longer be any certainty about the reality of Baptism, Confirmation, or the ordination of deacons, priests, or bishops.

A century later, St. Augustine would tackle this heresy. He dedicated the first fifteen years of his ministry as bishop to writing a number of works on the topic, explaining that the ministers of the sacraments are simply instruments, while it is Christ himself who acts in them through the power of his death and resurrection. Augustine's conclusion is contained in a pithy phrase: "When Peter baptizes, it is Christ who baptizes; when Paul baptizes, it is Christ who baptizes; when Judas baptizes, it is Christ who baptizes!" (*Tractatus in Ioannem* 6.7)

Donatism quickly gained a substantial following, especially in Numidia. Many synods were held to deal with this question, and the emperor Constantine got involved as well. Constantine had no theological background and behaved inconsistently, issuing condemnations followed by edicts of tolerance, as he would do later in regard to the Arian heresy.

Except for a small colony in Rome, Donatism never spread beyond Africa, but it met with astounding success in its country of origin, thanks to the personality and organizational genius of Donatus. He combined unyielding perseverance in the struggle against his enemies with diplomatic accommodation toward potential adherents to the sect. For example, he himself contradicted the fundamental Donatist doctrine of the invalidity of the Catholic sacraments when this would have caused particular difficulty, and although he had an orthodox conception of the Trinity, he began to incorporate the theory of the subordination of the divine Persons in order to befriend and add to his ranks the Arians, who were condemned at the Council of Nicaea in 325.

When Monica was born in 331, Numidia was overrun with this religious struggle, but her parents gave her a Catholic education. The town of Tagaste was relatively isolated and peaceful, safely out of the reach of theological disputes. But roadways linked the town with the great cities where the battle was raging full force: Madaura to the south and, above all, the capital, Carthage, to the north. Today, on the hills where the town of Tagaste once stood, sits the town of Souk-Ahras, which is located in modern-day Algeria on the border with Tunisia.

In the Roman period the region was exceedingly fertile. The Mediterranean climate fostered the extensive growth of vines and olive trees, and grain harvests were abundant. Tagaste was certainly not the most important town in its region. If it had not been the birthplace of Monica and Augustine, posterity probably would have forgotten it. Tagaste's origins go back to the very first years of the Christian era. Rome had imparted its genius to the construction of the town, granting to the municipal council the title *illustrissimus*. On the basis of this Roman identity—which, in its wise and legendary tolerance, accommodated the individuality of local culture—the preaching of the Gospel had spread throughout the city Christian values of fraternity and love toward the least fortunate, whom the pagan way of life tended to marginalize.

Monica's temperament reflected all of the characteristic elements of her early surroundings: the tenacity of her Punic ancestors, the equilibrium and diligence of the Romans, and the tenderness of Christian charity.

CHAPTER II

A Virtuous Child

We do not know the names of Monica's parents. According to the tradition found in the breviaries of the Augustinian Order, her mother was called Faconda, but this name appears nowhere in Augustine's works. Clearly they were observant Catholics, and they certainly would have resisted the Donatist schism. The Lord had great plans for Monica, and filled her with his gifts.

> ...[F]or she did not fashion herself or bring herself up: you created her, and not even her father or mother knew what kind of child would be born from them. She was brought up to reverence you, schooled by the crook of your Christ, the shepherd's care of your only Son, in a faithful family that was a sound limb of your Church.[7]

These are Augustine's words of praise for his grandparents, Monica's parents, who offered to the growing girl a family environment suitable for the development of Christian virtue.

Families of a certain means frequently had domestic servants who had grown up within the household; they maintained a tradition, faithfully fulfilling their duty to the point of scrupulosity. These servants were serious and totally dedicated to their masters, respecting them and receiving their respect in return, enjoying unconditional esteem and fulfilling the most delicate and sensitive tasks. In the house of Monica's parents, there was a servant woman who had grown up in the family of her paternal grandparents; this woman had been nursemaid to Monica's father, and now, in her advanced age, she was given charge of Monica and her sisters (we do not know how many siblings Monica had, or what their names were). She was to raise the girls according to the strictest standards, and because of her age—and especially her upright conduct—she enjoyed the full trust of their parents. Severe with herself, she was also severe with the children entrusted to her, often becoming overbearing. She did everything, however, with the intention of educating the girls in virtue and self-mastery. She trained them in sacrifice, especially as regards food, since the rest of their lives were already fairly well regulated. She did not permit them to take any food or drink outside of the meals they ate with their parents, and even these were frugal. In those hot, sun-drenched regions, abstaining from drink during the day was no small sacrifice, yet the strict "nanny" imposed it on her girls. Wine was absolutely forbidden. "Only when you get married," she told them, "and are put in charge of the supplies and storage areas, will water become distasteful to you, and you will acquire the habit of drinking wine." This might seem like fastidiousness and unnecessary severity, but any upbringing intended to form a solid and virtuous personality cannot ignore sacrifice, never as an end in itself but as a form of training the will to be ready to meet any situation in life.

Her education made Monica strong and fearless in her struggle to surmount the difficulties she would later face.

If the old servant woman decisively corrected every one of the girls' failures, she was also wise, loving, and prudent in her teaching and advice. She was a fervent Christian, and she instilled in Monica and her sisters a Christian view of life, reverence for the prayers and customs of the Christian community, and love for the poor. The accounts contained in the Augustinian breviaries about Monica praying through the night, sneaking out of the house to go to church, and depriving herself of food in order to give it to the poor are legends. But given her good natural disposition, the work of grace, and her upbringing, it is likely that she made quick strides toward holiness even as a little girl.

As would eventually be the case for Augustine, Monica's conscience was so delicate that in her latter years she would recount to her son things that she considered shameful failings, although these may well produce a good-natured smile from the modern reader. For instance, Monica's parents had given her the job of drawing wine from the casks in the cellar and bringing it to the table, because they knew that she was a sober and virtuous girl. Forbidden fruit tends to exercise a unique fascination on the young. Why should she not be able to say that she, too, had drunk wine? It was something reserved for her elders, which was precisely why trying some herself became so attractive.

Monica may have been virtuous, but she was still weak enough not to be able to resist this temptation. She began by barely touching her lips to the flask; then, sipping a little more each time, she got to the point of gulping down almost a whole glassful. The only witness to her actions was another servant who accompanied Monica to the cellar. Shortly afterward, a disagreement arose between the two for reasons we do not know. In the course of the argument, the servant hurled in Monica's face the epithet *meribibula,* meaning "wine-swiller." Instantly ashamed of herself, Monica acknowledged her fault. So great was her humiliation that she decided to quit her bad habit immediately. So, as St. Augustine later wrote,[8] God providentially used the argument with the servant to eliminate from Monica even this fault. She became an irreproachable child: serious, modest, obedient, gentle, full of attentiveness and concern for others. Her character continued to be formed by the operation of God's grace, by her wise upbringing, and above all by the effort she herself made to profit from everything her parents and teachers imparted to her.

What appears before us, then, is a noble spirit united with a tenacious will for which nothing was impossible. Fortitude, nobility, and decisiveness must not be confused with pride. Monica recognized her limitations and strove to improve her character, without seeking convenient excuses to conceal the truth. Authentic humility is truth, and the most radical truth is that everything good comes from God and not from our own merit. This awareness did not cause Monica to lose heart; rather, it permitted her to count upon God's help to overcome every obstacle, especially during the difficult years of puberty and adolescence. No one is born a saint, and Monica was no exception. From the very first years of childhood, her holiness was the result of continuous growth and cooperation with the grace of God.

She turned toward young adulthood after serene and fruitful years during which the main outlines of her personality had been traced, giving good hope for the future.

Chapter III

Marriage to Patricius

One of the greatest concerns for parents during ancient times was that of finding a husband for their daughters. They often did so without exercising very exacting standards, in order to avoid the shame of seeing their girls remain unmarried. St. John Chrysostom[9] effectively describes the sleepless nights of certain fathers who could not find peace until they had seen their daughters married.

Monica's parents, although good Christians, were not exempt from this social pressure. Their daughter had no reason to envy anybody else; if it is true that interior beauty is reflected on the outside, we can imagine Monica had a gentle and pleasing appearance. More importantly, she was adorned with excellent qualities of mind and heart, which must have made her interesting and attractive. Her conversation was lively and insightful, as we will later see during the period spent at Cassiciacum, and her company would certainly not have been boring.

Which of the men of Tagaste or the surrounding area would have the good fortune of marrying her? Her parents ultimately decided upon Patricius. While no precise information about his background seems to exist, biographers have suggested that he belonged to a family of decayed nobility. He was somewhat older than Monica and was a pagan, as many still were at that time. Could Monica's parents not have found someone better for her? A distance of sixteen centuries can make it seem that they should have done so, but the considerations that influenced their decision are ultimately unknown. Perhaps they were thinking only of social stature, physical attributes, or other factors that escape the historian.

As for the age difference between Monica and Patricius, the Augustinian breviaries and an apocryphal letter attributed to St. Augustine[10] give numbers that seem exaggerated. These sources claim that Patricius died at seventy-three years of age. As his death occurred in the year 371, that means he would have been born in 298, making him thirty-three years older than Monica. The same sources say that Monica was married at thirteen, lived as a wife for twelve years, and was a widow for sixteen years after her husband's death. The only precise figure here is the last one. The others are simply not feasible, because Augustine was born in 354, and therefore Monica would have had to have been married to Patricius, at the moment of his death, for at least eighteen years. Moreover, if we add up the three periods of Monica's life (her marriage at thirteen, then twelve years of married life, and sixteen as a widow), she would have been forty-one years old when she died, while Augustine says that she died at the age of fifty-six.[11]

Even if it is theoretically possible that Monica was married at thirteen, it does not seem likely that she would have had her first son, Augustine, after ten years of marriage.

Keeping in mind both these considerations and tradition's insistence on the age difference between the couple, the most probable conjecture seems to be that at the time of their marriage, Monica was around twenty years old and Patricius was a little over thirty.

Overlooking the age difference, why did Monica's parents give her in marriage to a pagan? A century and a half earlier, their countryman Tertullian had lashed out against mixed marriages, describing in his effective and direct style their sad consequences:

> If these things are so, it is certain that believers contracting marriages with Gentiles are guilty of fornication, and are to be excluded from all communication with the brotherhood, in accordance with the letter of the apostle, who says that "with persons of that kind there is to be no taking of food even".... Let us now recount the other dangers or wounds (as I have said) to faith, foreseen by the apostle; most grievous not to the flesh merely, but likewise to the spirit too. For who would doubt that faith undergoes a daily process of obliteration by unbelieving intercourse? ... Any and every believing woman must of necessity obey God. And how can she serve two lords—the Lord and her husband—a Gentile to boot? For in obeying a Gentile she will carry out Gentile practices—personal attractiveness, dressing of the head, worldly elegancies, baser blandishments, the very secrets even of matrimony tainted.... But let her see to (the question) how she discharges her duties to her husband. To the Lord, at all events, she is unable to give satisfaction according to the requirements of discipline; having at her side a servant of the devil, his lord's agent for hindering the pursuits and duties of believers: so that if a station is to be kept, the husband at daybreak makes an appointment with his wife to meet him at the baths; if there are fasts to be observed, the husband that same day

holds a convivial banquet; if a charitable expedition has to be made, never is family business more urgent. For who would suffer his wife, for the sake of visiting the brethren, to go round from street to street to other men's, and indeed to all the poorer, cottages? Who will willingly bear her being taken from his side by nocturnal convocations, if need so be? Who, finally, will without anxiety endure her absence all the night long at the paschal solemnities? Who will, without some sus-picion of his own, dismiss her to attend that Lord's Supper which they defame?[12]

While these pointed words may seem somewhat rigorous, there still remains the undeniable truth that marriages between a Christian and a non-Christian are fraught with difficulties for religious observance. In fact, disparity of religion is an imped-iment to Christian marriage. Marriage involves a complete sharing of everything that one is and one has; it is a total com-munion of life. For a Christian, faith cannot be considered after everything else—beauty, health, attractiveness, wealth, social position.... Of course, Paul does say that "the unbelieving hus-band is made holy through his wife" (1 Cor 7:14), but this requires an even greater degree of holiness, tolerance, and spir-it of sacrifice.

It may be said in defense of Monica's parents that in their time things were different than when Tertullian was writing. They were living in the post-Constantinian era, and a reversal of fortune had transpired for both sides: the number of Christians had grown considerably, and many pagans remained unbelievers only out of laziness. The Augustinian narratives indicate that Patricius was a tolerant pagan who not only did not oppose Christianity but even looked upon it with some appreciation. The only thing he lacked was an act of formal adherence, which he put off not out of intellectual principle but to avoid a more austere form of life. He wanted to continue practicing vices that Christianity did not permit. Monica's parents must have believed that their daughter was rooted firmly enough in her Christian convictions and the practice of virtue that she would be able to win over her husband. Eventually this did happen, although at the cost of much sacrifice.

From the viewpoint of Monica's parents, Patricius would have been commendable chiefly because of his social position, even though this was not accompanied by any great economic resources. Possidius[13] says that Augustine's parents belonged to the class of the *honestiores,* the upper class of Roman society, as distinguished from the *humiliores,* or plebeians. The *honestiores* enjoyed certain legal privileges as well, especially in regard to penal law. They could not be sentenced to be whipped or to work in the mines, nor could they be condemned to death, except under very unusual circumstances, and even then they could not be crucified or thrown to wild animals. Patricius held the position of "decurion" of the illustrious municipality of Tagaste. Decurions were municipal councilors originally recruited from among former magistrates on the basis of their land holdings and their age, which could not be below twenty-five, although exceptions were frequently made. Decurions were appointed for life. Since Patricius does not seem to have been wealthy, we can imagine that the fortune that permitted him to become a decurion must have declined over time.

By the late imperial age, the office had become an unavoidable burden, because it carried with it an "inheritance." The decurion's authority in administrative affairs was rather limited, yet at the same time he was saddled with personal responsibility for the municipality's tax receipts, which were often paid out of his own pocket. This put Patricius in the uncomfortable position of needing to maintain a certain

standard of life because of his social position, while secretly
tightening his belt in order to carry on. In essence he was
nothing more than a minor landholder barely able to survive.
When delusions of grandeur persuaded him to send his son
for advanced studies, he had to accept the charity of a rich
friend and fellow citizen, Romanianus, because the sacrifices
he and Monica were able to make toward his son's education
would never have been sufficient.

As for Patricius's character, he had the passion of a
Numidian; he would pass from moments of tenderness and
affection, in which he appeared entirely dedicated to his wife
and children, to moments of uncontrollable rage, in which,
losing sight of reason, he would become brutal and verbally
abusive. He was especially dominated by a powerful sex drive.
Augustine inherited this from his father and would engage in
a pitched battle against it until the time of his conversion. It
was Patricius who noted Augustine's "ripening sexuality" one
day when he took his son to the public baths, later boasting
gleefully of his discovery to Monica. Although Augustine
offers nothing but the highest praise for his mother in the
Confessions,[14] he writes about his father almost as if he was a
stranger and provides a glimpse of Patricius's lewd conduct
even within marriage. Hoping in his conversion, Monica tol-
erated even his marital infidelities.

This was the man with whom Monica shared almost
twenty years of her life. At times she demonstrated an authentic heroism that would be rewarded only at the end, when she
would see her husband convert, receive baptism, and die in the
arms of the Church.

CHAPTER IV

A Christian Wife and Mother

Monica's position in Patricius's house was anything but simple. She was beginning a new family, but in Roman law family was not as we understand it today. It included everyone (wife, children, and servants) under the patriarchal authority of the *pater familias*. His absolute power and command over life and death had been only slightly mitigated by three centuries of Christianity, during which the Gospel message had slowly and patiently transformed consciences from within and introduced new values. Yet the husband was still considered the master, and although the wife managed the house and had immediate responsibility for the servants, she remained in a state of subordination.

Monica could not have found her marriage to be easy; humanly speaking, it would have been difficult to share her life with a man prone to anger and unfaithful to his vows. She had been trained in sacrifice from her earliest years, however, and so she embraced marriage and family with a sense of mission. She armed herself with patience and endurance, serving her husband tenderly. Thus she slowly transformed her marriage into a far better relationship than other marriages with a more ideal starting point.

Patricius's elderly mother also lived in his house. He was probably her only child, or in any case her most affectionate. As can happen, she grew jealous of her daughter-in-law. Newlywed life is difficult enough without a third party stirring up trouble between husband and wife. Monica suffered greatly from this new living arrangement, but she quickly succeeded in turning to good the proverbial hostility between mother-in-law and daughter-in-law.

At first the servants incited Patricius's mother against Monica with malicious gossip and calumnies. They were prejudiced against the young mistress of the house and could not abide her managing the household affairs, although she did so with agreeable courtesy. They further reasoned that fostering discord between mother-in-law and daughter-in-law would work to their advantage. When things went wrong within the household, they thought to shift the blame to one or the other. But they underestimated Monica's temperament and virtue. She succeeded in winning over her crotchety mother-in-law with the "weapons" of gentleness and kindness.

The more the servants accused Monica of having spoken ill of her mother-in-law, the more she showed herself to be attentive and mild toward the older woman, never losing her patience. The more her mother-in-law grew irritated with her, the more Monica demonstrated respect and love in return.

One day the old woman, who was certainly not stupid, had simply had enough; she went to her son Patricius and told him of the servants' spiteful behavior.

Patricius responded by having the servants whipped. With this radical measure he put an end to a situation that was disrupting the peace of the entire household. Afterward, Monica's mother-in-law severely warned the servants that they would receive the same punishment in the future, should they ever again dare to speak badly of her daughter-in-law.

Monica had triumphed through her humility and practical wisdom; from that day on, relations between the two were more loving than if Monica had indeed been her own daughter, of such sweetness and mutual good will that they amazed everyone and made a lasting impression on the town of Tagaste. The servants, too, learned to appreciate Monica, slowly exchanging their bitterness for grudging and ultimately affectionate respect.

Her relations with Patricius were more difficult. Although Monica fulfilled her duty as a wife with dedication and tenderness, her husband could be arrogant, impetuous, carnal, and violent. It was difficult even to engage in conversation with him. At times, when Monica was not able to speak to Patricius directly, she tried to communicate with him through her actions. She served him with devoted love; Augustine notes that her greatest aspiration was to win her husband for Christ. She endured his faults in the hope—even more, in the trusting certainty—that she would one day see him become a Christian, and thus made righteous and chaste. When he verbally lashed out in anger against her, she did not respond in kind. Although she might have been tempted to lash back at him, Monica refrained from saying anything that might further provoke his wrath. Gradually his anger blew over and he calmed down. After the episode had passed, Monica would then approach her husband and calmly present her thoughts and opinions. She knew the art of choosing the right moment. She did not allow herself to be provoked by a situation, ruining everything by acting in the heat of emotion. But she did not reject confrontation, either; nor did she passively accept injustice, which might have led her husband to think he was always right. She was a competent strategist, gradually leading Patricius toward truth and goodness by means of a certain innate psychology, but above all through her patience and virtue.

In Book Nine of his *Confessions,* Augustine writes that there were many women in Tagaste who were married to husbands of a "gentler temper," but whose faces nevertheless bore the marks of blows and other signs of physical abuse. Such appalling occurrences were unfortunately all too common in the culture of that time. When Monica and the other wives would meet, they would talk together about their domestic misfortunes. Monica's friends could not understand why her face was never bruised. After all, everyone knew about Patricius's nasty temper. These women reasoned that if their husbands, who were milder in temperament, were so quick to raise their hands, Patricius was even more likely to leave marks of anger on his wife's body. Monica responded to their questions by reminding them in a "joking vein" that their marriage contracts constituted legal documents that effectively made slaves of them. As such, she advised them to remain in a subservient position and not openly defy their husbands.

Familiar as we are in our society today with the evil of domestic violence, it is difficult to view this kind of advice as an appropriate way of dealing with such a situation.

Again, it must be remembered that women in Monica's time had few rights and little recourse in correcting or improving the conditions in which they lived. Yet Monica had found a way to work as best she could with a reality she could neither control nor change. So she shared these words with the other women in order to make her bitter medicine more palatable. Then she revealed her strategy of letting Patricius blow off steam and later finding the right moment to reason with him. Augustine remarks that the women who followed her example were happy with the results, while those who did not continued to be mistreated by their husbands.

Monica worked to establish peace with everyone. Augustine affirms[15] that God gave his mother the great gift of being a peacemaker; she had the ability to calm discords and smooth over misunderstandings. She refused to repeat anything she may have heard one of her friends say against another, aware that when the spirit is disturbed because of injured pride, anger, or envy, one often gives vent to exaggerated and rash words. She shared with the persons in question only what might encourage reconciliation. Everyone knew that they could find in Monica an understanding and reliable confidante, an adviser possessed of intelligence and insight, whatever the situation.

While this was due to the gifts God had given her, it also came from Monica's own effort to better understand herself and others, so that she might grow in Christian love. She desired everyone to be happy and to live in peace. To that end, Monica spared none of her time, resources, or energy in trying to be an instrument of peace—not a false peace, based on manipulation and lying, but the authentic peace that comes as a gift from God and results in justice.

Although she had to suffer a great deal and her marriage was certainly not among the happiest, Monica also experienced great consolations, especially through the birth of her children. Few earthly joys can compare with the exhilarating experience of parenthood, of transmitting the gift of life to one's children.

Patricius became a father when he was in his forties. He must have delighted in holding his first child in his arms and kissing him tenderly. Over the years, Patricius would prove to be a proud and boastful father. Wanting his children to be better than everyone else, he would spare no expense or sacrifice for them; he expected his children to bring him glory and economic prosperity in return. Monica, for her part, must have felt unspeakable joy bringing her children into the world. She saw them as great gifts of God and dreamed of educating them in the profound ideals of the Gospel, illustrating with her own life the example that her children would follow day by day.

Monica gave birth to two sons and one daughter. It seems certain that Augustine, who was born on November 13, 354,[16] was her first child. Her other two children, of whom we find traces in Augustine's works[17] and in the biography of him written by Possidius,[18] were Navigius and Perpetua.

Although we do not know precisely when Navigius's baptism took place, we do know that he had already received the sacrament when Augustine was preparing to be baptized by Ambrose of Milan. Navigius would follow Monica during her voyage from Tagaste to Rome, Milan, and Ostia. He appears above all at Cassiciacum and at Monica's deathbed. Through scanty references from Augustine's writings, we glimpse a mild and peaceful temperament. He certainly did not possess Augustine's fire and vitality; just as Navigius did not follow his older brother in his youthful excesses and deviations, neither did he seem to share the extent of Augustine's ardor as a new convert. Later Navigius would refrain from joining his many friends who were embracing the monastic life, choosing instead to marry and have children. His two daughters would grow up and enter the religious life. It also seems that he had a son named Patricius, who became the sub-deacon of Hippo. Navigius appears to have been a good family man who lived an ordinary life, in which he never gave anyone particular reason either to blame or praise him.

Perpetua's name does not appear in Possidius or in the works of Augustine but in tradition. We hear accordingly that she married, was widowed, and then entered the religious life. Elected superior of a monastery for women in Hippo, which Augustine himself had founded, she held the responsibility for many years. In Agustine's Letter 211, which was addressed to the religious sisters of Hippo and includes in the fifth chapter the monastic Rule of Augustine (probably reproducing the earlier *Rule for the Servants of God*), Augustine spoke of these religious women as his consolation in the midst of his many burdens as a bishop. He also wrote against symptoms of laxity that had been cropping up, recalling the examples of holiness his sister left when she was the superior of that same monastery. So Perpetua occupied an important place as the immediate executor of Augustine's directives in the religious life in one of the first monasteries of the West.

Among other things, Monica is praised for raising her children in Christian faith and sanctity. The fruits of the teaching she imparted to these three fortunate children blossomed fully in their adult lives: Augustine's sanctity is recognized by the entire Church; Navigius, a faithful, ordinary Christian, formed children who dedicated themselves totally to the Lord; and when Perpetua died, she left behind a legacy of holiness in Hippo. With love and devotion, Monica had created an atmosphere of true Christian sanctity in which to nurture her family.

CHAPTER V

The Pious Widow

Patricius would not live to see the honor his children would bring to him. He died in 371, while the seventeen-year-old Augustine was a student in Carthage.

By means of her intelligent, tactful, and patient activity, Monica had succeeded little by little in cultivating her husband's unruly character. The passing of years must have played a part in making Patricius wiser, more serene, and less impulsive. Living with Monica for almost twenty years could not help but have had an influence on him. Patricius may have been volatile and moody, but deep down he had a good heart. The words Monica spoke at just the right moments engraved themselves more and more deeply upon his mind; but more important still was her example and heroic patience, which over the years pried Patricius's heart wide open. In his wife he saw the incarnation of the sublime values that the Christians preached. He read in her face the joy and serenity that his paganism and his vices had never been able to bring to him. He discovered within her soul a tremendous strength that could not be solely of her own doing. In a word, through Monica he encountered and personally touched the divine.

Conquered by grace, Patricius made his first great step toward Christ and the Church by enrolling himself in the catechumenate. It was not rare at that time to find men his age among the catechumens; many put off baptism indefinitely in order to avoid assuming all of the commitments and demands of Christianity. Then, when these persons felt the approach of death, they hurried to ask for the sacrament of regeneration.

This is what the great Emperor Constantine had done a little more than thirty years earlier, as had many others who had chosen to remain catechumens for their entire lives. Augustine himself was a catechumen from the time of his birth until the age of thirty-three; and Ambrose, Basil, Gregory Nazianzen, and John Chrysostom prolonged their catechumenate until they were adults. Although it was then common to receive baptism as an adult, the Fathers of the Church argued against the habit of delaying baptism until the moment of one's death, an attitude that to them smacked of cowardice.

For Patricius, an illness that would prove fatal finally convinced him to receive baptism. After everything she had endured from her husband, Monica—who at forty years of age was in her full maturity—now joyfully anticipated sharing with him her lifelong faith, participating together at the table of the Lord, and giving a common testimony of Christian life. She must have felt less isolated as she looked forward to the fulfillment of the great ideal of Christian marriage, imitating the love that exists between Christ and the Church and facing together, in a spirit of faith, the various problems of life. They could provide a better example for their children and would become a family open to welcoming others, especially the most needy. Then, suddenly, all of these desires and plans vanished like a dream. Death took Patricius precisely when a life happier in every way was about to begin for them. Monica accepted this painful separation; in her profound faith, she knew Patricius had been saved and was living in the Lord. In a short while she too would be reunited with her husband in the glory that transfigures all human realities.

After the prayers and the Mass for the deceased, which were already in use at that time, Monica buried Patricius in Tagaste. He rested in a tomb in which she had also reserved a place for herself, so that the two bodies that had been united in life would be close together after death, awaiting the resurrection. But divine Providence would arrange things differently.

Although she still had to provide for the children who remained in her care, Monica did not consider remarriage an option. Augustine, the eldest, was only seventeen years old and needed to complete his higher studies in order to become a rhetorician; Navigius and Perpetua were still children and thus incapable of providing for themselves.

The social provisions in place today were unknown in antiquity. Unless they owned property that provided a sufficient income to survive on, widows were typically plunged into poverty. Patricius's inheritance was not large enough to provide economic peace of mind. Monica placed her trust in the help of God—resolved to make the sacrifices necessary in order to complete the education of her children—and embarked upon the state of widowhood with courage.

Widows were held in particular esteem in the ancient Church, and those who strove to remain unmarried received a special consecration. This led to the creation of a distinct category within the Church that brought with it particular duties for widows, as well as a commitment on the part of the Christian community to support them. This form of consecration, however, was not an option in Monica's situation: she was still young, being only forty years old when Patricius died, and she still had adolescent children at home. She therefore had to take on the sacrifices of widowhood without the benefit of assistance.

It is likely that in order to provide for Augustine's studies, Monica had to accept the discreet generosity of Romanianus, which she tried to repay by acting as a mother for his son, Licentius, whom we will meet again at Cassiciacum.

Augustine paints an interesting picture of Monica as a widow.[19] She embraced an even more sober and austere way of life and consecrated herself to the Lord in complete chastity. She needed little to live on, refraining from fashionable dress and fasting frequently. Everything that she, in her poverty, was able to save, she gave away as alms. She was dutiful toward the presbyters and the heads of the Church, humbly serving and seeing Christ in all those who found themselves in need because of sickness or any other reason. She participated in the celebration of the Eucharist each day, bringing her own offering to the altar. She also went to church each morning and evening to be with the Lord, to hear his voice in Sacred Scripture and in the priests' homilies, and to lift up her own voice to him in fervent prayer.

Monica exemplifies the portrait that St. Paul sketches for widows, fulfilling all of the conditions for being a true widow, that is, carrying out the particular role acknowledged for her within the Christian community.

In essence, Monica lived a life of prayer and charity, harmoniously blending the two ideals of Martha and Mary: action and contemplation. She drew from prayer the breath she need-ed for her spiritual life and the energy necessary for works of charity. After contact with her neighbor, she returned willing-ly to the Lord, knowing well that only he could resolve certain situations. Above all, she looked to the Lord for the desire clos-est to her heart: the conversion of her son Augustine.

Apparently Monica's children did little to help their mother and relieve her of her problems. Rather, they added to her worries. Augustine, in particular, broke through all moral barriers and, ignoring restraint, gave himself over to every sort of intellectual, religious, personal, and social expe-rience. For Monica, his behavior was a cause of ongoing anx-iety and concern.

CHAPTER VI

The Son of So Many Tears

Monica's glory will endure through the ages above all because she gave the great St. Augustine to the Church and the world. But this gift was the fruit of a life replete with tears.

She had brought him into the world like any other child, amid the sufferings of labor, but the sufferings of her spiritual labor were immensely greater. Augustine put it this way:

> I can find no words to express how intensely she loved me: with far more anxious solicitude did she give birth to me in the spirit than ever she had in the flesh.[20]

Augustine used this idea of spiritual childbearing on other occasions. It effectively captures the intense attention with which Monica followed her children and their friends:

> She had brought up children, in labor anew with them each time she saw them straying away from you. Finally, Lord, she took care of all of us who were your servants—for by your

gift you permit us to speak—who before her death lived together as companions in you after receiving the grace of your baptism; she took care of us all as though all had been her children, and served us as though she had been the daughter of all.[21]

When Augustine was born, the practice of baptizing children, though defended doctrinally, was not actually widespread. In Africa, Tertullian had recommended delaying baptism until a child was old enough to know Christ.[22] Cyprian, half a century after Tertullian and one century before the birth of Augustine—appealing to the Council of Carthage held in the autumn of 253—maintained that the mercy of God should not be denied to anyone who has been born.[23] He also rejected the opinion of Bishop Fidus, who said that baptism should not take place before the eighth day after birth in order to maintain a parallel with circumcision.

Monica did not have Augustine baptized—not because she was neglectful of the spiritual formation of her children or weak in faith. Monica wanted Augustine to understand his baptism and receive it after a long and intense period of preparation. For this reason, she had enrolled him in the registry of catechumens when he was still a little boy. Augustine himself wrote about the symbols of the catechumenate he received as soon as he was born:

> While still a boy I had heard about the eternal life promised to us through the humility of our Lord and God, who stooped even to our pride; and I was regularly signed with the cross and given his salt even from the womb of my mother, who firmly trusted in you.[24]

Enrollment in the catechumenate signaled that membership in the Church was not far away. The enrollment would be followed by instructions given by the bishop or presbyter to those making this journey of faith and intensified with daily meetings during Lent before the catechumen's reception of baptism at Easter. Remnants of these instructions, which were called *ad illuminandos,* are found among the writings of the Fathers of the Church during this period. There are the *Catecheses* by Cyril of Jerusalem, the *De Mysteriis* (On the Mysteries) and *De Sacramentis* (On the Sacraments) by Ambrose of Milan, and the *Baptismal Catecheses* of John Chrysostom. Augustine himself would give wise guidelines for the instruction of catechumens in the *De Catechizandis Rudibus* (The First Catechetical Instruction), which he wrote in reply to a request from the deacon Deogratias of Carthage.

Monica did not expect others to take care of that first and most important duty of parents: the education of their children. For her, education meant above all leading her children to the Lord. Augustine found his first catechist in her; from her he drew the name of Jesus Christ together with the milk that he sucked.[25] And he never forgot this name, even amid the darkest and stormiest moments of his life. When he was seemingly won over by the works of profane writers—for example, Cicero's *Hortensius*—he never felt fully satisfied, because he did not find in them the name of Christ, which his mother's instruction had rooted deeply in his heart.

One can imagine the tenderness with which Monica, holding her baby on her lap, spoke to him of the things at the center of her life: the love of the Father, the incarnation and redemption of Christ, the immense dignity of being a child of God and belonging to his Church, and the eternal triumph prepared for us in paradise. All of this came with a naturalness that imprinted the truth and beauty of the faith in a sweet and lasting way upon the heart of her son, molding him like clay.

No one can ever completely reject the instruction received from one's mother; even for those who consciously try to do so, there remains in the depths of one's soul an undercurrent that reemerges of its own accord and forms the basis for a return to the ideals learned during childhood. None of the many philosophical doctrines that Augustine embraced were ever able to convince him of the non-existence of God or divine Providence.[26] He was unable to accept the philosopher Epicurus, whose teaching he had considered and then immediately rejected, because Augustine had a firm faith in the immortality of the soul and the future judgment.[27]

Later in life, after having wandered about seeking the truth and coming to understand the falsehood—or at least the insufficiency—of human doctrine, Augustine would find the strength to return to God through

> ...that religion which is implanted in us in our childhood days and bound up in the marrow of our bones. She indeed was drawing me unknowing to herself.[28]

To ensure a Christian upbringing for her children, Monica had to deal with the obstacle of her husband, who was a pagan. She succeeded in making her house a believing home, and in instilling in her children's hearts faith in Christ. She made up for Patricius's parenting deficiencies by doing all she could to see that God became the father of her children.

> My mother did all she could to see that you, my God, should be more truly my father than he was, and in this endeavor you helped her to win the argument against a husband to whom she, though a better person, was ordinarily subject, for in taking this course she was in fact subjecting herself to you, who so commanded her.[29]

Augustine was about seven or eight years old when he developed an intestinal blockage that endangered his life.

Moved by the faith that Monica had instilled in him, he asked both his earthly mother and Mother Church for baptism. Monica, torn by sorrow yet more concerned for her son's eternal salvation than for his physical well-being, hurried to make all the preparations. The Sacraments of Initiation were usually celebrated at the Easter Vigil, but in cases of extreme necessity, such as when a catechumen was in danger of death, baptism was administered immediately. Augustine, however, suddenly recovered from his grave illness, and since he was no longer in danger of death, his baptism was postponed. He would later complain of this in his *Confessions,*[30] asking why such a wonderful mother would delay his purification. But for Monica, baptism was too important and demanding; already knowing the fiery temperament of her son, she foresaw the passions that would be unleashed in him and the vices into which he would fall during his youth. Once baptized, his sins would be much more serious. So, in accordance with the practice of her day, Monica decided to delay baptism until the image of God would be better formed within her son and errors and vices would no longer defile him.

In the meantime, Monica and Patricius enrolled the child Augustine, who demonstrated from his earliest years a lively and promising sharpness of mind, for studies in Tagaste. Like all children, he did not enjoy going to school because of the effort study required. The teaching methods of the time did not leave much room for creativity or inventiveness but were based mainly on memorization and imitation. Coercive measures in response to any negligence in study or discipline were the order of the day.[31] Augustine remembered with terror his days spent in primary school, the *ludus litterarius,* and the many whippings he received from his teacher:

I would be beaten whenever I was lazy about learning. This punishment was taken for granted by grown-up people and many a pupil had undergone it before we did...so my stripes were laughed at by my elders and even my parents, who would not have wished anything bad to happen to me. But bad it was, and very dreadful for me.[32]

So even Monica, according to the pedagogy of the time and to the Bible's teaching that "those who spare the rod hate their children" (Prov 13:24; cf. 29:15), accepted corporal punishment as a means of education. This scholastic environment led Augustine to hate the subjects he studied, especially Greek, which he never fully assimilated, although he did find a certain enjoyment in studying Latin.

His father's pagan influence manifested itself in Augustine's relations with his peers through his bullying and lies. Notwithstanding this, he also had many gifts of intelligence and insight, and for this reason, Monica and Patricius were not content with his primary schooling in Tagaste. They sent him to Madaura, seventeen miles south of Tagaste, for his secondary, or "grammar," studies. Because he was still a child to Monica, it was difficult for her to be separated from him, and she did her best to provide for him through friends in the area. Unlike Tagaste, Madaura was not a calm and isolated place. One breathed the "big city" atmosphere in the schools, the squares, and the theaters. His attendance at the theater especially began to exert a negative influence on Augustine's sensitive spirit. He felt burning within him the feelings and emotions described in the works that he studied, and so the crisis of adolescence began.

Augustine returned from Madaura at the age of fifteen. He had profited intellectually from his grammar studies, but his spirit was restless and vulnerable to the passions of youth. He spent his sixteenth year—a truly disastrous period for him—in Tagaste, waiting for a decision about the continuation of his studies. The fires of adolescence coursed through his veins; and, with neither study nor work to keep him busy and help channel this energy, he gave free rein to his passions, living in the kind of indolence that leads to vice.

Monica had not yet understood her son's struggles, and she believed him to be innocent and naive. Patricius, who had been a catechumen for a short time, had a much better understanding of his son's situation and began to speak to his wife of her responsibilities of guidance and vigilance. By the time Monica finally opened her eyes to the truth about the situation, she was seized with fear that her son, even though he had not yet been baptized, might go down the wrong road, never to return. Augustine acknowledges that his mother's words resounding in his ears were the same words God later used when he called Augustine back to himself.[33] At that point, however, the youth considered his mother's warnings as merely the worries of a fussy old woman and, glorying in his developing sexuality, continued recklessly along his way. Monica counseled him to abstain from illicit sexual relations with women and especially from adultery, but in despising his mother he despised God himself and fell headlong toward the abyss. He began to seek out immoral company. With these "friends" he was not ashamed of his sins but of his behavior when it was not as brazen as theirs.

Although concerned about her son's chastity, Monica did not consider channeling his sexual impulses by contracting for him a legitimate marriage, which at that time was frequently celebrated at a young age. As he wrote in his *Confessions,*[34] Augustine would have agreed to this solution, but his parents had something quite different in mind.

Patricius was aware of his son's virility and was already eager-
ly anticipating grandchildren, but he claimed that marriage,
although perhaps satisfactory in some regards, would compromise the future of such a promising young man by
abruptly interrupting his studies. Monica also wanted
Augustine to continue his education, but for different reasons
than her husband's. Patricius was hurriedly gathering money
to complete his son's studies in Carthage—an end he intended to achieve at any cost. His ambition for Augustine to
appear better than everyone else was uppermost in Patricius's
mind, and for this he submitted to greater sacrifices than
many of his more prosperous but less ambitious fellow citizens. Monica took another point of view. She also made
sacrifices for her son's studies, not to obtain earthly glory
through him but solely for the sake of his own good. She cor-
rectly believed that her son's greatness would proceed from
his knowledge. True knowledge ultimately brings one closer
to God, who is Truth. So the more her son studied, she reasoned, the more he would learn the truth and begin to walk
along the right path. This is what eventually happened, of
course, although various hardships arose along the way.

In 370, when he was seventeen years old, Augustine went
to Carthage to begin higher studies in rhetoric. Although she
was glad to see him moving forward in life, Monica was
anguished to let him go. Circumstances proved she had every
reason for concern. When she had said goodbye to him before
he left for Madaura, she had felt a mother's anxiety for his tender years. Now he was going even farther away, into the midst
of so many physical and especially spiritual dangers, which
were particularly tempting because of Augustine's unbridled
youthful passions. Monica intuited the storms that were about
to assail and shipwreck him.

Patricius died during that scholastic year, and although Monica remained a widow, she continued to help provide for her son's studies.

Carthage, the great capital city of Africa—with its splendid monuments commemorating its glories, the intense merchant traffic, the bustle of the streets and the forum, the famous theaters, and the circuses with their provocative exhibitions—was tailor-made to provide a hedonistic and unruly life for the provincial Augustine. Additional negative influence came from the scholastic environment, replete with students whose only interest was to amuse themselves and wreak havoc throughout the city. If Augustine was looking for trouble, he quickly found it.

He became captivated by a woman he met in Carthage, and in 372 she bore him a son. The boy's name was Adeodatus. This, then, is what had become of Monica's advice: illegitimate sexual relations, concubinage, and a child outside of marriage. But this was not Monica's greatest sorrow. She was crushed when she learned that her son had become an active member and supporter of the Manichaean sect. She wept more than mothers do over the physical death of a child.[35] For her, in fact, the spiritual death into which her son had fallen was more terrible than physical death. In the deep faith and supernatural illumination God granted to her, she saw the situation clearly and bathed the ground with tears in every place she went to pray. The Lord did not despise her many tears and would ultimately grant her prayers.

Manichaeanism was the religion founded by Mani (215–274) in Persia. It was a mixture of various philosophical, religious, and mythological beliefs: from Zoroastrianism it took the fundamental dualism between good and evil that dominates all of creation; from Buddhism it took certain norms of behavior; from Christianity it took the concept of messianic redemption; from Gnosticism, the doctrine of the various "aeons" or spiritual powers evolved by progressive emanation from the eternal Being; from Neo-Platonism, a few touches of pantheism and mysticism. To constitute a society, the Manichaean religion needed a firm organizational and hierarchical structure, so it was divided into two classes: the "elect," who were able to embrace a strict ascetic rule of life, and the *auditores* or "hearers," who supported the elect with alms and various works.

Augustine found in this sect an answer to many of his questions, an answer he would later see as false. The Manichaean religion satisfied his materialism; for the Manichaeans, who were dualists, material was evil and was associated with the evil creator god; the good god was immaterial. Augustine also found in Manichaeanism the solution to the problem of evil, which had been bothering him for some time, with its twofold principle—good and evil—of creation. He found an answer to his problem regarding the "immorality" in the Old Testament, which the Manichaeans had solved in the same way the Marcionists did, by creating their own canon of Scripture. Above all, he found that the Manichaean religion perfectly suited his own personality, which was divided between lofty ideals and base passions.

Finishing his studies in Carthage in 374, Augustine returned to Tagaste with his lover, whose name he never revealed, and their two-year-old son, Adeodatus.

Monica would have been willing to extend a mother's welcome to all three of them and seek a solution for their irregular situation, but the heresy into which her son had fallen held her back. If the Apostle John had given the instruction to avoid even greeting a heretic in order to steer clear of participating in that person's evil works (cf. 2 Jn 10–11), how much less could one make room for a heretic in one's home? The fact that she, who loved Augustine more than anything else in the world, had arrived at such a point shows how tragic the situation was.

Augustine was forced to ask for hospitality from Romanianus, his wealthy patron, whose easygoing logic led him, together with some of his friends, to sympathize with the Manichaeans. A terrible period followed. Monica found no peace and would have died of a broken heart if God had not comforted her as only God knows how to do. One night, Monica had a hard time falling asleep, but as soon as she dozed off, God showed her in a dream the wonders he had prepared for the future. In her dream Monica was standing on a piece of wooden timber, afflicted and weeping. Suddenly a luminous and smiling young man drew near to her, asking why she was sad. She explained that the loss of her son's faith was the cause of her tears. The young man said to her, "Why are you crying? Don't you see that where you are, he is there as well?" And turning around, Monica saw that Augustine was standing on the same plank with her. The dream then ended. In the morning, she ran to her son and excitedly told him about it. Augustine was so infatuated with his new belief, however, that he explained the dream by predicting that his mother would become a Manichaean! But Monica had the certainty that comes from the Lord and she rebutted her son's interpretation, maintaining that the young man had not told her, "Where he is, you also will be," but rather, "Where you are, he also will be." She clung to the belief that her son would return to the faith she had instilled in him.

Augustine misled everyone with his false doctrines, but not his mother. Although Monica had not studied, her mind was sharp and penetrating, and above all she had the help of God. She remained firm in her Catholic faith, the standard that guided every aspect of her life. Augustine continues:

> The dream foretold, so long in advance, the joy in store for this devout woman many years later, and so gave her comfort in her present anxiety. Nearly nine years were to follow during which I floundered in the mud of the deep and the darkness of deception, often struggling to extricate myself but crashing heavily back again. Yet throughout these years my mother, a chaste, God-fearing, sensible widow of the kind so dear to you, though more eager in her hope was no less assiduous in her weeping and entreaty, never at any time ceasing her plangent prayers to you about me. Her pleas found their way into your presence, but you left me still wrapped around by the fog, and enveloped in it.[36]

After her prophetic dream, Monica welcomed her son back into her home with full confidence that he would return to the Catholic faith. Meanwhile, Augustine had to find a way to support the woman he was living with and their son, Adeodatus. He soon opened a school in Tagaste. Although teachers at that time barely managed to scrape together a living from their few paying students, Augustine had no other choice. He would begin modestly before becoming a famous teacher.

When he returned home each day, his mother would greet him lovingly but avoid any doctrinal discussion, knowing her son's proficiency in philosophical argument. She realized that it would take a person as learned as he to convince him of his error. So she began to look for authoritative, cultured, and pious men who would be able to speak to him and bring him back to the right way. She was not at all ashamed of being perceived as troublesome in her search; above everything else she had the spiritual well-being of her son at heart.

One day Monica learned that a bishop named Antigonus was passing through Tagaste, and she went to visit him. Tagaste did not currently have a bishop in residence, although it had been an episcopal see in the past and would become one again in 394 under Alipius, one of Augustine's closest friends. For the time being, however, the nearest bishop resided in Madaura, probably Antigonus's original home. When Monica went to meet him, he would have been an old man if he was the same Antigonus who had participated at the Council of Carthage in 349.

Monica explained her son's entire situation to the bishop. He apparently had already heard about Augustine, who was famous throughout the province on account of his speeches and public debates, from which he always emerged victorious. His pious mother insisted that the bishop should meet with her son and convince him of his errors. The bishop responded with great prudence, and Augustine later acknowledged that he had acted wisely. Antigonus remarked to Monica that it was not only a case of a doctrinal dispute with someone arrogant and unwilling to listen to others; Augustine was a brilliant speaker who had already confounded capable and educated men. Rather than confront the young man prematurely, the bishop suggested that Monica be patient and wait. Using no other weapon than prayer, she would one day see her son finally realize his error and return to sound principles. Monica, however, was not satisfied with these words and began again to weep and even to beg the bishop to do something for her son. Then, to reassure and encourage her, the bishop confided to Monica that as a child he had been entrusted by his mother to the Manichaeans. By reading and copying all of their books, he had fallen into the errors of that sect but later had emerged from them. This would happen for

Augustine as well. Still Monica persisted. Finally the venerable bishop lost his patience and, weary of her nagging, brusquely told her: "Go away now; but hold on to this: it is inconceivable that he should perish, a son of tears like yours."[37]

Monica received these words as if from heaven. She took them as another sign that the Lord in his goodness had granted to encourage her in her ceaseless prayer and copious weeping. The bishop's words were indeed an extraordinary summary of Monica's life: a life of tears for the conversion of her son. And her tears were so insistent and prolonged that God could not remain unmoved by them.

CHAPTER VII

On Augustine's Trail

In Tagaste, Augustine was deeply affected by the death of a close friend. This young man had been lured into believing the fables of Manichaeanism by Augustine himself, who was his peer and exercised a certain influence over him. Then, falling seriously ill, Augustine's friend was baptized a Catholic. When the man recovered, Augustine assumed he would not attribute any importance to the baptism he had received while ill and would continue to consider himself a Manichaean. Yet, when Augustine began to joke about his friend's baptism, the man issued a sharp warning: if Augustine wanted to continue their friendship, he must not speak of the matter again.

A short while later, this same man suffered another attack of fever and died. Augustine lamented the sorrow that plunged him into such a downcast state that, wherever he looked, he saw nothing but death and could find no peace. In Book Four of the *Confessions,* he describes at length this episode and the state of mind to which it brought him. For the very first time he had met with the failure of his Manichaean propaganda and conquests, and the lesson he had received from his friend burned deeply within his soul.

After this event, Augustine was unwilling to remain in Tagaste, where everything reminded him of his dead friend. He moved back to Carthage. As he had attained a certain measure of fame, it was not difficult for him to open a school of rhetoric in the capital. His mother, always fearing for his spiritual well-being, felt it necessary to be nearby. At the cost of significant sacrifice, she followed Augustine to Carthage. From that moment on, her life would be comprised of trailing after her son throughout Africa and Italy. Ignoring her own needs, she dedicated herself entirely to his good.

In Carthage Augustine wrote his first work, *On the Beautiful and the Fitting*. It dealt with the beauty inherent in things and was a first step toward his landmark theme: uncreated Beauty. If she had read it, Monica could not have been unmoved to see in this work her son's penetrating mind and good dispositions, which would guide him in his search for truth.

Overall Augustine did not find great comfort in Carthage. His students were certainly not of the caliber a teacher would hope for; they were undisciplined, had no desire to study, lacked seriousness, and agreed with one another only in making mischief, which ranged from childish infractions to criminal matters. Augustine was forced to endure his pupils' increasingly disruptive behavior. Unable to tolerate the situation for long, he decided to teach somewhere else. He had heard that students with greater seriousness and commitment were studying in Rome, and so he decided to establish himself in the glorious, ancient capital of the Empire. Augustine also made no effort to hide the fact that he was attracted by the thought of acquiring a better financial situation.

Perhaps the truest reasons for Augustine's move are known only to the Lord, who used this journey to provide the meetings and circumstances that would bring Augustine to conversion. In any event, Monica wept bitterly when she learned that her son was about to leave. She assumed that Rome would provide further occasions of error and temptation for her son. Just as he was beginning to have doubts about Manichaeanism and was distancing himself from it a bit, she now feared he would go plunging into other errors. Augustine had, in fact, discovered errors in Mani's teaching about the stars, and from this he had started to lose faith in his infallibility. Presumptuous mistakes in mathematically measurable things indicated the possibility of mistakes in everything else. Gnawed by doubt, Augustine realized that, in the end, the Manichaeans were seeking to destroy others' systems of belief rather than justify their own. His meeting with the Manichaean bishop, Faustus, renowned for his fame, eloquence, and piety, proved the last straw, as even Faustus could not answer Augustine's many questions.

Monica trusted that Augustine would soon be converted and did not want him to be separated from her. If he determined to depart for Rome, she was just as determined to go with him. Augustine did not appreciate such maternal interference, but since he respected and loved his mother, he resorted to deception rather than direct confrontation in planning his departure. He told her that he was going to the port to say good-bye to a friend. Monica didn't believe him; she responded that she would accompany him and would not return without him. Augustine pointed out that the wind was not blowing and so the ship would not be able to depart for the time being.

He convinced her to wait and spend the night in a little church dedicated to St. Cyprian that was located near the port. In the meantime, Augustine would spend time with his departing friend. The proposed solution seemed reasonable to Monica, because she found her joy in recollection and prayer and also because she would be able to check from time to time to see if the boat was leaving. But while she was in prayer, accompanying this as always with abundant tears, something must have happened. Perhaps she lost track of time or was caught up in the Lord and let go of all other thoughts, or maybe she simply fell asleep. Whatever the case, prior to dawn the wind began to blow and swell the sails, and Augustine boarded a ship that quickly put out to sea, losing sight of the shore.

His strategy succeeded. When Monica left the little church that morning and realized she had been deceived, she thought she would lose her mind in her anguish. She turned again to the Lord with lamentation and weeping. Reflecting on this episode in his maturity, Augustine saw in it an intervention of Providence for his good and for the good of his mother:

> You took no heed, for you were snatching me away, using my lusts to put an end to them and chastising her too-carnal desire with the scourge of sorrow. Like all mothers, though far more than most, she loved to have me with her, and she did not know how much joy you were to create for her through my absence. She did not know, and so she wept and wailed, and these cries of pain revealed what there was left of Eve in her, as in anguish she sought the son whom in anguish she had brought to birth. Yet when she had finished blaming my deception and cruelty, she resumed her entreaties for me, and returned to her accustomed haunts, while I went to Rome.[38]

It was the year 383 when Augustine arrived in Rome, and he was twenty-nine years old. He stayed in the home of a

Manichaean, since he had not yet officially broken ties with that sect. Rome was still the capital of paganism, but three centuries of Christian history had had an effect upon it, and its face was changing. Many bishops who had been called together for the synod of the previous year were still present; they had assembled to come up with a solution to the schism of Antioch. The See of Peter was occupied by Damasus, a wise, learned, and holy octogenarian. At the Pope's side was Jerome, whom he had hired as a biblical consultant and secretary. Jerome had come to Rome in the company of the head of the ultra-Nicene faction of Antioch, Bishop Paulinus, who had ordained him to the priesthood a few years earlier. As Augustine traveled the streets of Rome, it would be impossible for him not to have come upon Jerome on his way to Aventine Hill. There Jerome had formed a biblical studies circle that drew the most prominent women of the Roman aristocracy; they would hang on every word that issued from that unsophisticated monk's lips. Members of the group included Marcella, Fabiola, Paola—with her daughters Eustochio and Blesilla—and many others.

This great and lively ferment of Christianity made a tremendous impression on Augustine, who was very confused and saw reasons for doubt wherever he looked. He ended up becoming a skeptic, an adherent of the philosophy of the Academics.

Soon after his arrival in Rome, Augustine had a serious attack of fever, which at first seemed would prove fatal. At this juncture he was certainly not considering baptism, as he had when he was a child. But the Lord could not leave him to die this way, with eternal death following his physical death. What would become of all the prayers and tears of his mother? What about the visions in which the Lord had reassured her that her son would return to his faith? Later Augustine would affirm that he did not doubt for an instant that his physical healing was granted through his mother's intercession in order that his spiritual healing might follow it.[39] The Lord could not disregard those prayers and tears, because Monica was not asking for gold, silver, or any good of this earth, but for the spiritual salvation of her son. Jesus had instructed his disciples to pray in this same way, with confidence that they would be heard:

> "Ask, and it will be given you; search, and you will find; knock, and the door will be opened for you. For everyone who asks receives, and everyone who searches finds, and for everyone who knocks, the door will be opened" (Mt 7:7–8).

Recovering from his illness, Augustine threw himself back into teaching, but this brought him little comfort. At first he was amazed at how many students he had. They were certainly not like the ill-mannered hoodlums he had instructed in Carthage. Everything went well with these new students until the time came to pay for their lessons, when they promptly abandoned their teacher and moved on to another school! One can imagine the precarious situation Augustine found himself in. It seems he may have been forced to accept more than basic hospitality from his Manichaean host. So although Augustine was no longer convinced in Mani's doctrines, prudence suggested that he continue in the company of the Manichaeans. This habitual way of living created further doubts within him. The asceticism the Manichaeans preached was merely an appearance, and sin was not at all foreign to them, as they claimed in their theories. All of the objections Augustine had tried to flee when he was in Carthage crowded back into his mind. These continued working deep in his conscience, especially his discussions with a man named Elpidius, who had explained to him how the Manichaeans used altered copies of the Scriptures. Even the doctrine of the Academics, which Augustine had learned through the philosophers Arcesilaus and Carneades, and toward which he was inclining at that time, ultimately consisted in doubting everything. Augustine's state of mind could not have been more confused.

His financial problems, touching his very survival, began to weigh upon him as he sought a better situation. The right opportunity came when the prefect of Rome, the fervent pagan Aurelius Symmachus, returned from Milan. There, at the court of Emperor Valentinian II, he had spoken in favor of reestablishing the altar of Winged Victory in the Senate. Among the duties he sought to carry out upon his return was sending a professor of rhetoric to Milan. Some influential Manichaeans suggested Augustine's name. After hearing Augustine give a trial speech, Symmachus was happy to send him to Milan, both because he had enjoyed the young man's oratory skills and because Augustine had a reputation as being anti-Christian. To the prefect of Milan, one of the last remaining pillars of pagan culture, Christians were a pervasive nuisance.

For Augustine it was a real triumph. Essentially a provincial outsider until that time, he had now been chosen by the greatest literary authority of his day to occupy a public office with an official imperial status. He also had finally gained economic security, because his stipend was both ample and guaranteed. With great exuberance Augustine departed for Milan, traveling the imperial roads with full freedom. It was the summer of 384, and the young teacher, not yet thirty years old, was embarking upon a brilliant career.

Meanwhile, Monica could find no peace away from her son and thought of him night and day. The occasional bits of news she received from letter carriers or persons sailing to Africa didn't tell her everything she wanted to know. She was unable to read his face or see into his heart. How far had he come in his passionate search for knowledge? Had the doubts that had been brewing in his mind led to a positive outcome? Was he on the path of truth, or had he taken a detour into some other intellectual adventure?

Mother that she was, she could bear it no longer. Without regard for her advancing age or for the difficulties and hardships involved in traveling at that time, she decided to set out upon her son's trail.

On the ship, when storms struck and all on board feared for their lives, Monica found the right words to console even the sailors, who more than the others understood the danger they were in and could tell stories of their escape from similar perils. She told them with absolute confidence that they would arrive safe and sound, because the Lord had assured her of this in one of the many visions with which he favored her.

Arriving in Rome after that dangerous voyage—during which she had characteristically spread serenity and hope around her—Monica experienced keen disappointment when she discovered that her son was no longer there. She must have felt the need to rest and regain her strength, but her desire to see Augustine again was so urgent that, without hesitating, she departed immediately for Milan. There she discovered that he was going to take possession of his official teaching post.

If voyages by sea were extremely dangerous in the ancient world, those by land brought with them every kind of discomfort: endless plodding, weariness, danger from brigands, eating in haste what little one could, sleeping as best as possible and not always under a roof. It was a genuine adventure that could prove a severe test even for a hardy young man, not to mention someone like Monica, already in her fifties and weighed down with sorrow, worries, and fasting. A mother's love, however, knows no bounds or weariness, and Monica's was made stronger and more persevering by divine grace. Armed more with love and hope than with physical strength, she reached Milan, where after two years of forced separation she was finally able to embrace her Augustine once more.

She certainly did not find him in the best state of mind and heart imaginable. Augustine had reached the point where he despaired of ever finding the truth.[40] Nevertheless, he sought to console his mother by telling her the good news that at least he was no longer a Manichaean. Monica did not react as Augustine had expected, by expressing her amazement and joy. She simply accepted the news as an ordinary turn of events. This was not the only grace she was expecting for her son. She had entrusted him to the Lord through her insistent prayers. She was certain, therefore, that he would soon take the more important step and embrace Catholicism.

In the meantime, she petitioned the Lord even more with prayers and tears to hasten the day of Augustine's full conversion, a day for which she had been waiting so many years.

CHAPTER VIII

Meeting St. Ambrose of Milan

In Milan, Monica found herself once again living under the same roof as her son. Between his studies and teaching, she had been constantly separated from Augustine, continually witnessing his departure, whether for Madaura, Carthage, Rome, or Milan. She was now determined that she would never again leave his side. She waited for him to return from his lessons, reassured him when anxieties flooded his mind, and never ceased praying for him.

Through God's mysterious plan, Monica, Augustine, and his entire family had arrived in Milan, where they would meet Ambrose, the man divine Providence had chosen to help Augustine. Ambrose had occupied the see of Milan for a decade, since the time when he had been elected bishop by overwhelming public acclamation.

Ambrose had been born and raised in a Christian family, and his relatives had shown him examples of holiness. When he was a boy, he saw his sister Marcellina receive the veil in Rome from the hands of Pope Liberius. Ambrose remained a catechumen. After his studies he embarked upon a career as an imperial magistrate together with his brother Satyrus. They were assigned as lawyers at the prefecture or district of the Praetorium of Italy, Illyrica, and Africa, which was located in Sirmio. Two years after their arrival, in 367, the prefect Vulcatius Rufinus was succeeded by Sextus Petronius Probus, who advanced the two brothers in their career. He first called them to become members of his council, then appointed them "councilors." In 370, Ambrose became a "councilor," or governor, of the province of Emilia-Liguria. It is not known where his brother Satyrus was appointed governor. In this new and important post, Ambrose distinguished himself by his careful administration of justice, his well-tested honesty, and other qualities he demonstrated in his capacity as governor. All of this quickly earned him the people's respect.

After the death of the Arian Bishop Auxentius of Milan in 374, Ambrose went to the basilica where the election of a successor would take place. He felt his presence might be required to prevent or quell the riots that were expected to erupt between the two highly emotional factions of Catholics and Arians. As events proceeded, those present became increasingly aware of the fact that Ambrose was the only one capable of handling the situation, and that he would be perfect for the position of bishop. After repeated attempts to remove himself from consideration, he was forced to accept the office.

St. Paul says that a neophyte should not be chosen as bishop, much less someone who hasn't even been baptized (cf. 1 Tim 3:6), and the Council of Nicea had prohibited elections by spontaneous acclamation.[41] But it was thought necessary to make an exception to these rules, as had been done in 236 in Rome for Pope Fabian, in 319 for Philoxenus of Antioch, in 362 for Eusebius in Caesarea, and as would happen in 381 for Nectarios in Constantinople.

Once he was made bishop, Ambrose felt the entire weight of the responsibility he had assumed and devoted all of his strength to meeting the challenge. He received instructions from the presbyter Simplicianus, who had prepared him for baptism and who would later succeed him as bishop of Milan. Ambrose delved into Sacred Scripture, which he studied day and night with the aid of the works of both the Greek and Latin Fathers. As he was not lacking in basic education, intelligence, and good will, he absorbed in a relatively brief period the wisdom he had been called to proclaim.

This was the man whom Monica and Augustine would encounter. Physically he was small of stature, thin, and somewhat cross-eyed, as can be seen in the fifth-century gold mosaic found in the chapel of St. Victor in the Basilica of St. Ambrose in Milan. That frail body, however, contained an energy capable of confronting the entire Empire. He had a quintessentially Roman sense of equilibrium, the prudence to wait for the right moment without falling into opportunism or compromise, and a truly uncommon understanding of the human soul that came from long experience. This temperament, combined with a sense of the beautiful and a sense of art, with nobility and refinement of sentiment, made him a true gentleman, a well-rounded man who attained perfection as much as was humanly possible. Completing the picture with the richness of Christian asceticism and the action of divine grace, one catches a glimpse of what Ambrose was like.

When Monica came to Milan, she began to listen regularly to his preaching. She had never heard the Word of God
explained with such precision and depth, such zest and sweetness. She simply could not wait to listen to this man of God
and give her spirit rest in abundance and delight. Monica considered Ambrose to be an angel sent from God, and she loved
him all the more when she learned that he was influencing
her son as well, opening to Augustine the beauties of
Christianity through his preaching, while illustrating them
concretely in his own life.

Since arriving in Milan, Augustine had wanted to visit
Ambrose. He did so not because he was friendly toward
Christianity, but because the bishop was one of the most
important persons of the Empire. He had prevailed over
Symmachus, blocking the restoration of the statue of Winged
Victory in the Senate. He had been the closest adviser to
Emperor Gratian, who had been assassinated the year before.
And now he held the greatest influence with Gratian's succes-
sor, his half-brother Valentinian II, who was only thirteen years
old and reigned under the supervision of his mother, Justina,
a fanatical Arian. Milan was the seat of the Empire, and
Ambrose, both in terms of his political importance and his
renown, outstripped even the bishop of Rome, the great
Damasus, and his successor, Siricius.

Augustine was naturally curious to meet Ambrose, who
was reputed to be a great rhetorician, and a meeting was
subsequently arranged. Although Augustine was not a
Christian, Ambrose nonetheless welcomed him like a father,
and his charisma quickly won over the young professor. For
Augustine, professional curiosity in the bishop gradually gave
way to interest in his message. Ambrose explained the Scriptures—particularly difficult passages of the Old Testament—in

a way that impressed Augustine. Slowly he grew to admire and love Ambrose, but with a sort of reverential fear that made him keep his distance, preventing the two from striking up a close and familiar acquaintance.

Because Augustine had been sent to Milan by Symmachus, the acknowledged leader of the pagans, Ambrose saw him in a certain negative light. Even after Augustine converted and Ambrose baptized him, their natures and experiences of life were so different that they never developed a deep friendship. In terms of temperament, Ambrose was serious, dignified, and prudent, while Augustine was fiery and impulsive. Ambrose had never been a slave of sensuality, having chosen to live a celibate life early on; Augustine had a woman at his side. Ambrose, who came from a senatorial family, had entered into an official role as a path marked out for him ahead of time; Augustine was a provincial, who had made his own fortune by using nothing other than his intellectual talents. Ambrose had a legal and practical mind, while Augustine was strictly an intellectual, intent upon the deepest philosophical problems and speculation. Augustine would naturally speak of Ambrose in his *Confessions,* but the bishop of Milan, who lived ten more years after Augustine's conversion and baptism—years during which the neophyte would become first a priest and then a bishop—makes no reference to him in his treatises or letters. And yet, for Augustine, Ambrose was an instrument of Providence.

As had already happened in Tagaste, Monica's maternal love eliminated any sense of hesitation she might have experienced about being intrusive and insistent in her quest for someone who could speak to her son and convince him. Ambrose was not spared from her pleading. But he was too busy with lofty duties such as Church Councils, imperial consistories, political affairs, embassies, the organization of assistance for the poor and the sick, and the composition of written works and homilies. It would have been difficult for him to spend extended time speaking with an individual, as was necessary in Augustine's case. When the young man went to visit Ambrose, he had to contend with a vast crowd of people, each with his or her own problem to present to the bishop. On the very rare occasions when Augustine caught Ambrose alone, he found him deeply immersed in reading and meditation. The saintly bishop did not even realize there was someone waiting at the door, which was always left open. Augustine was not intrusive like his mother, and he did not dare disturb the bishop during the only moments he was able to dedicate to study and personal reflection. He would wait for Ambrose to raise his eyes and give him a signal to approach—but this never happened. After watching him a little while, Augustine would tiptoe away, leaving the bishop's residence with his problems still weighing him down. Although no enlightening conversations had resulted, his visits were not completely useless; simply being in Ambrose's presence was enough to exert a positive influence on Augustine and dispose him favorably toward the action of divine grace.

Conversions are not often the result of discussions and debates. They are the triumph of example. In the confused jumble of the human heart there are mechanisms that remain unmoved by the iron laws of logic, while they journey to places that could never have been reached by reasoning alone.

Through the mysterious influence that emanated from Ambrose, Augustine was drawn to listen to him by a mixture of curiosity and inexplicable attraction. It was precisely the preaching the bishop addressed to the great crowds filling the basilica that made Augustine's objections to the Christian faith fall one by one. There was nothing childish here, nothing incoherent; rather all was harmonious and sublime. The result was that Augustine's conversations at home with his mother had a common point of reference: Ambrose's discourses interested them both.

Monica quickly became familiar to Ambrose. He always saw her in one of the front rows, displaying an attitude of composure and recollection that was in no way affected, but was the natural reverberation of a deep and sincere interior piety. He began to connect this image of the mother with that of her son as well. He was greatly impressed by Monica's fervor at the services and by her deeply religious behavior. So gradually, when he saw Augustine as he was going from place to place, Ambrose would stop for a moment to sing her praises and congratulate him on the good fortune of having such a mother. Augustine would respond courteously to the compliments, almost tempted to take advantage of these brief moments to bare his soul to the holy bishop. But knowing how busy Ambrose was, Augustine's words died upon his lips and his questions retreated into his heart. At this point, the doubt that afflicted him was itself something positive, a necessary step toward complete healing. Augustine's search for truth under the influence of Ambrose lasted approximately two years.

Meanwhile, the bishop's struggles in the Church in Milan were reaching their peak over the matter of the basilica, which the Arians were demanding for themselves. The imperial mother, Justina, had never been reconciled to the fact that after the death of Auxentius in 374, the Milan church no longer belonged to the Arians. She had schemed to establish at least one Arian bishop there in addition to the Catholic bishop. The tumultuous events that followed the death of her husband, Valentinian I, with constant threats from barbarians and usurpers to the reign of his half-brother, Gratian, had given her little opportunity to carry out her plan. Toward the end of 384, she felt that his position was established solidly enough for her to make a power play.

The Arian bishop, Mercurius, arrived in Milan. Theodosius, emperor of the East, had deposed him from the see of Durostorum, in Romania. Mercurius's presence in Milan was precisely the pretext the empress had been waiting for to once again demand a basilica for the Arians. She probably asked for the Portian basilica, which was located outside the city walls. Ambrose refused and was called to appear before the imperial consistory. A large crowd of the faithful had preceded him, threatening to riot, so the court was forced to give in. Justina tried other methods; she moved with her court first to Aquileia and then, after returning briefly to Milan between the end of 385 and the beginning of 386, to Pavia. By this means she tried to keep Ambrose at a distance in order to diminish his power. But Ambrose steadfastly refused to hand over the church, and even went so far as to close himself up within the Portian basilica together with the faithful.

In March of 386, the court returned to Milan, and imperial troops were sent to surround the basilica. Since the faithful needed to remain continually indoors, it became necessary to occupy their attention and keep them from getting bored, so Ambrose divided his time equally between preaching homilies, giving commentaries on the various books of the Sacred Scriptures, and singing. He introduced the antiphonal singing of the psalms and composed a number of hymns, many of which became famous and were later incorporated into the celebration of the Divine Office.

As always, Monica was among the first ranks of the faithful present to defend the rights of the Church and bolster the position of the courageous bishop. She enjoyed Ambrose's warm and inviting eloquence, and she sang the songs with all her heart. She would later teach these same songs to the young men gathered around Augustine in Cassiciacum.

These were days of great uncertainty, but also of an intense Christian experience; the faithful of Milan discovered what it meant to be a community and what their bishop meant to them. As a widow in Africa, Monica had already formed the habit of going to church each day, and she felt that she was part of the Christian community, considering it a family. With a figure such as Ambrose, she felt more intensely the joy of shared prayer and fellowship, and she even provided food for those who remained in the basilica for days at a time. To find herself in the company of Ambrose, to have the opportunity to speak with him, to profit from his profound teachings, and, together with other Christians, to fight against the excesses of imperial power, was for her a magnificent experience of the living Church.

The imperial forces made a number of efforts to dislodge the resisters, but Ambrose always responded with courage, ready to die rather than give in to intimidation. After a while, the soldiers themselves began to enter the basilica to join those who were praying and singing there. In the end, the empress was forced to back down, and on Holy Thursday, April 2, 386, she ordered the troops to withdraw. Ambrose and the Church in Milan had won, and Monica had also played her part. Their exultation was tremendous.

Throughout her stay in Milan, Monica tried to follow all of Ambrose's directives. She believed him to be the representative of God as well as her spiritual father, even though obeying him sometimes involved renouncing herself and her own habits. For example, in Africa it was customary on the anniversaries of the deaths of martyrs to honor them by bringing bread and wine to their tombs and sharing these with the poor. Monica observed this practice diligently and with great devotion, even in Milan. But one day while she was bringing food to the tombs of the saints, a guard at the cemetery turned her away, telling her that the bishop explicitly prohibited this practice. As soon as she heard that this order came from Ambrose, Monica made no effort to oppose it; for her, his voice was the voice of God. Thus she provided an example of how to receive instructions from pastors who, illumined by God and with the grace of their state, offer such teaching or guidelines for the pastoral good of the faithful. Actually, the reason Ambrose had issued the prohibition was because of the danger of superstition inherent in these customs, which imitated the pagan feasts. They were established in the belief that the dead needed to eat and were consoled when their relatives performed this act of piety. The practice also led to drunkenness for some persons, who went from tomb to tomb, making toasts at each one.

This was not even remotely the case for Monica, the pious widow; she intended only to make a symbolic gesture in honor of the martyrs and to provide food for the poor. In her confirmed sobriety, she merely moistened her lips with the cup of wine, which, moreover, was always mixed with a large quantity of water. Here Monica realized that Ambrose was giving a general directive. So for the sake of obedience and the good of all, she sacrificed her devotion, purifying it and maintaining the good intention from which it had arisen. She continued to visit the tombs of the martyrs regularly, bringing…not a basket full of the fruits of the earth, but a heart full of more purified offerings, her prayers. In consequence she was now able to give alms to the needy, and it was also possible for the sacrament of the Lord's Body to be celebrated at these shrines—and fittingly, since it was in imitation of his passion that the martyrs offered themselves in sacrifice and were crowned.[42]

As Augustine notes, Monica's immediate obedience was another sign of her devotion and veneration for Ambrose, in whom she saw the instrument of salvation for her son.

Another of Monica's customary practices when she was in Tagaste was fasting on Saturdays. In Milan, however, Christians ate normally on Saturdays. Monica wasn't sure what she should do. Augustine was personally not concerned about such matters, but seeing his mother's anxiety, he wanted to ease her burden and went to Ambrose about the situation. The bishop responded:

> What else can I recommend to others than what I do myself? …When I am here I do not fast on Saturday; but when I am at Rome I do: whatever church you may come to, conform to its custom, if you would avoid either receiving or giving offence.[43]

This wise response indicates Ambrose's prudence as a pastor. When it is not a question of doctrine or precise instructions from Christ, any practice that is not intrinsically evil can have arguments both for and against it. It is the responsibility of pastors to establish what is best to do in certain circumstances, depending upon the persons and the situation. Wherever one goes, one leaves behind the practices of one's place of origin and adopts those of the new place. This is what Paul did, becoming a slave among the slaves and a Scythian among the Scythians. So also Monica, who was certainly not deficient in her sense of ecclesial practice, accepted all of the customs of the Church in Milan, even when this meant breaking with habits that had been instilled in her since childhood. When Augustine told her what Ambrose had said about her fasting question, she was satisfied and immediately put into practice the bishop's instructions.

Monica's participation in the occupation of the Portian basilica illustrates her deep involvement in the Christian community of Milan. She did not consider herself an outsider, knowing well that the Church of God is spread throughout the earth and that Christians are fellow citizens together with the saints and brothers and sisters of one another. She participated fully in the joys, sufferings, fears, and hopes of the Church in which she found herself. Augustine was aware of what was happening in the Christian community, though from a certain distance. He recounts how moved he was hearing the singing of sacred hymns in church and witnessing the amazing things that happened through the work of Ambrose.

Shortly after the victory at the Portian basilica, Ambrose had received a private revelation from the Lord, in which he was shown where the holy martyrs Gervasius and Protasius were buried. The faithful joyfully celebrated the solemn procession of these venerable relics to Ambrose's basilica. Monica, always among the most fervent, rejoiced together with her bishop for the generosity of the Lord, who in this way had highly favored Ambrose for the persecutions he had suffered on the Lord's behalf.[44]

CHAPTER IX

Toward Augustine's Conversion

"The pure of heart will see God" (Mt 5:8). By far, one of Augustine's greatest problems was his passions, especially that of sensuality. He describes himself during this period in the following way: "I was hankering after honors, wealth, and marriage...."[45] His brilliant intellect ranged across vast expanses of thought. Ambrose constantly gave him starting points for reflection, and he became increasingly aware of the inconsistency of the ideologies through which he tried to resolve the problems of life. He understood more and more that the gift of complete truth comes from Christ. But he couldn't make up his mind. There were too many ties binding his heart, too many forms of slavery weighing upon his will, and he didn't have the strength to set himself free. His vision was blurred, and he could not see God.

Through her prayer, Monica was already daily hastening the conversion of her son. Moreover, as a wise and prudent woman, she also made concrete efforts to prepare the way for this event. As long as Augustine had a mistress, he could never receive baptism, even if he wanted to. So Monica took steps to resolve the situation. The most logical solution would have been for Augustine to marry the woman who had been at his side for fourteen years, whom he loved tenderly, and from whom he had received the gift of his son, Adeodatus. Yet the marriage never happened.

Instead, this woman had to separate herself from the man she had loved and faithfully served for so long. After having stood by him through trials and difficulties, she now returned to Africa with the firm resolution never to marry. One cannot but be moved by profound pity for this woman forced to ignore her feelings and break away from the life she knew; it must have been an agonizing decision for her. The separation brought anguish to Augustine as well; he acknowledges that his heart was torn open. The wound would not heal until his conversion.[46]

How did this happen? How could Monica have been so cruel and insensitive toward her son and his companion? Augustine does not give an exact answer to this, so all the historian can do is guess. Some have suggested that the woman was already consecrated to God when she joined Augustine, and so the marriage could not have been celebrated. If this were the case, the bishop would have been able to release her from her vows. Other scholars conjecture that there might have been contingent reasons, such as finances, or some other earthly motive.

The most probable hypothesis is the existence of an objective, unalterable impediment based on the laws of the time.

The *Lex Iulia de Maritandis Ordinibus* banned Roman citizens from marrying certain kinds of women, such as freed slaves and actresses. Because of these prohibitions, men increasingly began to take mistresses instead of marrying. This sort of concubinage probably explains the situation between Augustine and his lover. If it caused him great anguish to send her away, and Augustine doesn't blame his mother or anyone else for this, it probably means the woman belonged to a social class that Roman citizens of a certain rank were prohibited from marrying.

Apart from the various hypotheses, the working of divine Providence is evident in this painful separation. Had he married at that moment, history would never have known the great bishop of Hippo.

Nothing further is said about the mother of Adeodatus. Augustine writes no more about her, nor does he ever reveal her name, since she must have been alive at the time he was writing. One hopes that she found peace and happiness in her chosen state. She was certainly stronger than Augustine if she was able to leave him and never give herself to another man. Augustine acknowledges that she was superior to him on this point; he was unable to imitate her. A slave of his desires, he soon felt the need to take another lover.[47]

The first step had been taken to clear the way for Augustine's baptism by dissolving a relationship that could not be ratified by marriage according to the laws of the time. Monica still saw marriage as one of the prerequisites for her son's baptism, knowing well that he could not live a celibate life. So she began looking in Milan for a potential bride from a good family. She found one, and Augustine was satisfied. He asked her parents for permission to marry her and received their consent. But the girl was not yet ready to be married; she was still "two years too young." Roman law stipulated that one had to be twelve years old in order to marry. By this calculation, the girl would have been ten at the time. Because of the great age difference, which would have made Augustine three times as old as his future wife, some authors think Augustine's use of the phrase "marriageable age" should not be taken in the literal legal sense, but may be understood to mean that two years were needed to get everything in order for the marriage to take place. Augustine would not wait; he simply could not live without a woman near him. So in the meantime he simply took another mistress to share his bed.

At the same time, he wanted to open a school of philosophy with the friends, who had followed him to Milan, and to seek the truth with them. But how could he do this with his spirit weighed down so heavily by the flesh? His best friend, Alypius, repeatedly told Augustine in no uncertain terms that he would never make any progress until he was able to free himself from his concupiscence. Alypius was a few years younger than Augustine; after studying under him in Tagaste and Carthage, he had preceded his teacher to Rome in order to study law. He then followed Augustine to Milan. After a few youthful transgressions in which he had let himself be carried away, Alypius now lived in complete continence. He presented to Augustine his own witness on behalf of that form of life that would facilitate the creation of a community dedicated to the things of the spirit. Augustine wanted to follow him but could not. His fleeting efforts always failed due to his weakness in the face of such overpowering desires.

In addition to Alypius, Nebridius had also come to Milan from Carthage for the sole purpose of joining Augustine. His benefactor, Romanianus, likewise came, as did other friends impelled by their enthusiasm for philosophy.

Augustine had made significant progress on an intellectual level; after leaving behind Manichaeanism, he also overcame skepticism, materialism, and naturalism. But victory over intellectual error was not everything. He still needed to win victory over his own passions. After reading the Neo-Platonists Plotinus and Porphyry, who gave him a much more spiritual idea of God than the Manichaeans had, he was ready for St. Paul. This reading, which harmonized and purified all the elements of truth he had previously acquired, opened the way for his long and complex conversion. By now it was simply a question of putting into practice what he already believed in theory.

In this state of mind Augustine turned to a highly respected priest of the Church in Milan, Simplicianus, who, as we have earlier seen, had instructed and guided Ambrose in the faith. Augustine opened his heart and shared everything stirring within him with this knowledgeable and holy man. Simplicianus was convinced that Augustine needed nothing more than encouragement and a few inspiring examples to change his thinking and lifestyle. So Simplicianus recommended Marius Victorinus, the great African pagan orator and translator of the Latin Neo-Platonist books that Augustine had also read. In his writings and speeches, this famous orator had previously mocked the Christian religion in every way possible, but as old age drew near he courageously converted and professed the Christian faith, disregarding the reaction of his pagan friends and benefactors. For the sake of his profession of faith, he was even ready to give up teaching and close his school when Julian the Apostate banned Christians from teaching in 362.

Conversation with Simplicianus made a deep imprint in Augustine's heart. A few days later he received a visit from one of his African friends, Ponticianus, who was in Milan on important imperial business. Ponticianus, a Christian, was extremely pleased to see the Letters of St. Paul on Augustine's table. While they were speaking together, their conversation turned to Anthony the Great, founder of anchorite monasticism, who had died thirty years earlier. Anthony had heard the voice of the Lord commanding him to sell all he owned, give the money to the poor, and follow him. He then found the courage to leave everything behind and go out into the desert to lead a life of prayer and penance.

After speaking of the conversion of Anthony, Ponticianus continued with the story of two high-ranking officials, friends of his, with whom he had gone walking in the countryside around Treviri. They had come across a hut where some monks were living, and his two friends had stopped there to talk with the monks while Ponticianus went on ahead. When he returned, Ponticianus found that they had firmly resolved to dedicate themselves to God through the monastic life, renouncing the emperor's good favor and the promising careers before them. They had also both been engaged to be married. When their fiancées learned what had happened, they too had entered a monastery.

These examples of conversion delivered the final blow to Augustine's rebellious will, sending him into such a state of agitation that he could do nothing but weep. He was fighting a difficult battle; on the one hand, he was attracted to the truth of Christ and the beauty of the Christian ideal, but on the other hand he saw himself defiled by the filth of his passions, a slave to pride, ambition, and especially lust. He vented his feelings with his faithful friend Alypius, saying:

> What is happening to us?... What does this mean? What did you make of it? The untaught are rising up and taking heav-

en by storm, while we with all our dreary teachings are still
groveling in this world of flesh and blood! Are we ashamed to
follow, just because they have taken the lead, yet not ashamed
of lacking the courage even to follow?[48]

It upset Augustine that he could not find the strength to act
decisively, always putting off his resolution until the next day.

While he was caught up in the grip of this terrible interi-
or struggle, he heard a sound coming through the window of
a house near the garden where he was. It was the voice of a
child, saying, "Take and read, take and read!" These words
could not have been spoken by accident. Augustine realized
God was speaking to him. He ran to the table, where he had
left the Letters of St. Paul, and opened a page at random. His
eyes fell upon the following words:

> ...not in reveling and drunkenness, not in debauchery and
> licentiousness, not in quarreling and jealousy. Instead, put on
> the Lord Jesus Christ, and make no provision for the flesh, to
> gratify its desires (Rom 13:13–14).

It was a direct answer from the Lord to his anguished questions. Augustine brought the book to Alypius, who read the
passage and continued to the first verse of the following chapter: "Welcome those who are weak in faith." Alypius applied
these words to himself since the preceding passage had not
applied to him, chaste as he was.

The grace of God had finally triumphed. Augustine was a
new man, and with Alypius he decided to change his life.

Who could have been more pleased than Monica to learn
of this event? Augustine didn't want to keep it to himself, but
rushed to share the tremendous news with his mother:

> We went indoors and told my mother, who was overjoyed.
> When we related to her how it had happened she was filled
> with triumphant delight and blessed you, who have power to

do more than we ask or understand, for she saw that you had granted her much more in my regard than she had been wont to beg of you in her wretched, tearful groaning. Many years earlier you had shown her a vision of me standing on the rule of faith; and now indeed I stood there, no longer seeking a wife or entertaining any worldly hope, for you had converted me to yourself. In so doing you had also converted her grief into joy far more abundant than she had desired, and much more tender and chaste than she could ever have looked to find in grandchildren from my flesh.[49]

Monica was the happiest woman in the world. An entire lifetime of tears and prayers had, by the grace of God, come to a happy ending. God had not been able to resist her constant and trusting appeals. During their later conversations at Cassiciacum, Augustine would turn to his mother and say:

Let us pray, therefore, not to receive riches or honors or any such fleeting, unstable things that come and go in spite of our best efforts, but to receive those things that make us good and happy. I entrust the happy realization of these desires above all to you, mother, since through your prayers I believe firmly and without any doubt that God has granted me the insight to place absolutely nothing before the search for truth, to want nothing else, to think of nothing else, and to love nothing else. Nor may I cease believing that, if you ask for it, I will obtain this great gift which I have begun to desire through your merit.[50]

And elsewhere, Augustine affirmed:

In my confessions, I explained how salvation was granted to me through the sincere tears that my mother poured out on my behalf each day.[51]

This was the culminating moment of Monica's life. She had lived for the sole purpose of seeing her son convert and become a disciple of the Lord; she would affirm this even in the face of impending death, during a lucid moment between attacks of fever. Hagiography and Church history both emphasize this relationship of Monica's praying and weeping for her son Augustine with the intention of bringing him back to the right way. Now, after all the prayers and sacrifices she had made, she finally knew that her dream had come true. It was one of those moments in life where heaven seems to be within reach; the joy one tastes at such a moment is an anticipation of eternal beatitude, a glimpse of the happiness God has prepared for those who love him.

One can only imagine the deep consolation Monica experienced. She witnessed the fulfillment of the prophetic words the bishop of Madaura had pronounced: "It is not possible that the son of these tears should perish." She tasted the goodness of the Lord, and her heart swelled with gratitude. Now she desired nothing else than to see the day of her son's baptism.

CHAPTER X

The Countryside of Cassiciacum

It was in August of 386 when Augustine made his decision to convert and leave everything behind, devoting himself entirely to God. One of the first things he would have to give up was his school, which continued throughout the summer months. Augustine prudently considered his course of action and decided he should not stir up a hornet's nest by suddenly abandoning his public post. He decided to wait the few days until the grape harvest vacation before saying good-bye to his students. As he suffered from asthma, he could allege health reasons for not taking up his lessons again when school reopened. In the meantime, he would make arrangements for someone to replace him.

There was also the matter of his fiancée, who was awaiting the day of their marriage. Although it is unclear as to how or precisely when it happened, the engagement was called off. In his *Confessions,* Augustine comments that Monica rejoiced so much in Augustine's conversion that she, like him, no longer desired a profitable marriage for him.

At this point, Augustine was free to inaugurate the group of friends who would dedicate themselves to philosophy and asceticism—a group he had long dreamed of. But how could this be done in the midst of the bustle of the city and the gossip that would circulate once people found out that Augustine had abandoned his old life in order to embrace Christianity? A friend named Verecundus, who was also a teacher of rhetoric, came to his assistance. Verecundus owned a villa in the Brianza area, almost twenty miles from Milan in a place called "Cassiciacum," modern-day Cassago.[52] He gladly made it available to his friends, regretting only that he could not be part of their group, since he had a wife and could not leave her or his teaching post. He, too, desired to become a Christian and would have liked to join Augustine's discussions about truth and goodness. Verecundus did become a Christian before his death two years later in 388.

Another of Augustine's dear friends, Nebridius, did not go with him to Cassiciacum. No precise reason is given for this; he remained in Milan for a few days with the intention of joining the group as soon as possible, but the delay continued, until finally Augustine and the others returned to Milan in order to be inscribed in the register of those to be baptized the following Easter. Nebridius had followed Augustine into Manichaeanism and astrology. He had left these behind before Augustine did, and was even one of the people who convinced him of its errors. The only remnant that his Manichaeanism had left behind was its Docetist conception of Christ, which meant denying the reality of Christ's Incarnation. Shortly after Augustine's baptism, Nebridius converted fully and received baptism himself. When he returned to Africa, he did not take up monastic life as did his friend, but he made efforts to convert his entire family, an endeavor that soon met with success. He had barely enough time to complete his mission before he died in 390 or 391, probably from an attack of tuberculosis contracted in Lombardy's unhealthy climate.

Except for Nebridius and Verecundus, all of Augustine's other friends were present in Cassiciacum. The group consisted of Augustine; Monica; Alypius, his faithful friend; Navigius, his brother, who was already baptized; Licentius and Trygetius, two of his students; Lastidianus and Rusticus, his cousins; and, finally, his son, Adeodatus, who was the youngest among them. Romanianus helped them generously as always by paying the expenses they incurred. He had a son named Licentius, a fiery young man little inclined to philosophy and religion; like Trygetius, he was one of Augustine's students who had taken up philosophy after leaving the military. Although Lastidianus and Rusticus weren't well educated, Augustine nevertheless admitted them to the debates, for which nothing more was needed than good sense and the capacity to reason.

Monica accompanied the group with the intention of overseeing the management of the house. More than anything else, hers would be a discreet presence at the side of her son, who was preparing to take the great step toward baptism.

While Verecundus's villa must have been something more than just a house in the countryside, including spacious accommodations and baths, there was nothing luxurious about it. It was precisely the atmosphere of simplicity and sobriety that Augustine and his friends were looking for. Especially useful were the grounds, with a generous lawn and trees that provided shade to sit under when the weather was good. In exchange for supervising the farmers of the estate, Augustine had permission to gather food from the gardens and the trees in order to reduce expenses.

The cooler air following rains that had extinguished the summer swelter announced autumn's approach. Ripe fruit hung from the trees, and mushrooms sprouted up in the moisture of the woods. The favorable season, together with the peace and tranquility of the countryside, encouraged introspection. It was the time to find rest and nourishment for the soul in meditation. Conditions were ideal for enthusiastic young men on the verge of making important decisions.

With her exquisite feminine sensibilities, Monica brought a much-needed touch of maternal affection and concern. She saw to the preparation of simple, wholesome food, took care of the rooms, and kept everything in order. She extended the love and service already directed to her son to his friends as well. Monica treated them as her own children, expressing as much concern for them as she did for Augustine. She had served her husband, Patricius, for many years and had always managed the house in Tagaste wisely and competently. Now she was responsible for overseeing the house in Cassiciacum, and she employed all of her experience and affection in the service of these young friends engaged in spiritual advancement and a search for truth. So great was her desire to contribute to the group's spiritual well-being that she spared none of her attention and concern, shouldering a burden of work and sacrifice that was by no means trivial. It had become second nature to her by now.

The young men had begun to read the psalms, which were the daily bread of Monica's prayer, and she explained them with simplicity and the depth of her lived experience. She taught them the hymns she had sung during the hair-raising hours of the occupation of the basilica and during the ordinary services celebrated in the church in Milan. In Augustine's *De Ordine*[53] we read that it was Monica who taught Licentius to chant the psalms. He liked the melody and went about singing to himself: *"Deus virtutum, converte nos, et ostende faciem tuam, et salvi erimus"* ("Restore us, O LORD God of hosts; let your face shine, that we may be saved," Ps 80:19).

Monica corrected the young man one night when she overheard him singing the refrain at the top of his lungs from an outhouse! It was not respectful, she told him, to sing the psalms in that situation. Licentius replied: "And if an enemy had trapped me in that spot, wouldn't God have listened to me?" The following morning he ran to Augustine and told him worriedly that he had sung holy things in an inappropriate place. Augustine's response was that God had certainly heard him and that the place was perfectly suited for sacred song, because God purifies us both physically and spiritually so that we can see his face.

During their gatherings as a group, Monica tried to transform all of their intellectual discussions into occasions of prayer. She was an expert guide in faith, somewhat like Mary with the Apostles in the Upper Room.

These were certainly among the happiest days of Monica's earthly life. She was living the ideal she had always desired; together they all formed a sort of family, without arguments and jealousy, but filled with the spirit of fraternal love. Their minds and hearts were united in pursuit of the true, the good, and the beautiful: everything that leads back to God as their root and source.

How she had longed throughout her life to see her son in possession of the truth! Now Augustine had not only attained it himself but was bringing others to it as well, and he showed great promise in leading many others to this truth.

Her heart was light again, and the nature of her prayer had changed from tears to praise, blessing, and thanksgiving to the Lord, who had not only fulfilled her wishes, but infinitely surpassed them. Those happy days spent in Cassiciacum were a foretaste of better "days" to come in paradise.

Prayer, listening to the Word of the Lord, meditation, fraternal sharing—all in an atmosphere of faith and serenity far from the maddening strife and the worries of the city—who could ask for anything more? For her part, Monica could have wished those days never to end, had it not been for her desire to witness her son's baptism and the baptism of those preparing with him for this blessed event.

CHAPTER XI

Monica the Philosopher

Monica, Augustine, and his friends spent six months in Cassiciacum, from September of 386 to March of 387. Though Monica preferred not to participate in the philosophical discussions—citing the excuse that she lacked education and was incapable of engaging in subtle disputations—Augustine insisted on her being there. Filial affection played a part in Augustine's admiration for his mother, but he also recognized Monica's sharp mind and her unique way of pursuing any type of question.

To borrow Plato's expression, Monica bore a love and a kinship with the truth found only in the pure of heart. She had reached the summit of philosophy, true wisdom, because God was reflected in the clarity of her soul as in a mirror. She saw things from God's point of view and knew how to discern between what is worthy, because it is eternal, and what is unworthy, because it is transitory. While Monica's contributions to the discussion were always simple, they were also both accurate and profound. Her words always revealed her interior richness.

The Cassiciacum dialogues show Augustine to be a great teacher with a fine command of the techniques of instruction. He masterfully directed the discussion, using the Socratic method to engage and put each of the participants at ease by permitting every person to express his or her thoughts in the best and most complete way possible. In this manner, he broke free from educational methods of his time, showing himself to be an authentic educator in the etymological meaning of the word (from the Latin *educere:* to draw something out from within). Augustine did not shape personalities according to a common mold, but encouraged each one to find his or her own autonomy and creativity. The transcripts of those exuberant and fertile discussions in Cassiciacum permit us to enter into the atmosphere of those days.

An important work that underscores Monica's genius and philosophical bent is *De Beata Vita* (*On the Happy Life*), a dialogue that continued over the course of two days, from November 13–15, 386.

November 13 was Augustine's thirty-second birthday (it is precisely thanks to this being mentioned in the dialogue that we know with certainty the date of his birth). Monica had prepared a light lunch for the occasion, as she did every day, so as not to weigh down the spirit or clip the wings of contemplation. After lunch, Augustine and the other eight members of the group—each individually named, with particular praise reserved for Adeodatus and his promising intelligence—met together in the area of the bathhouse. The question they faced was that of happiness: Where does it come from? How can one attain it? Augustine began from the nature of man as a com-

posite of soul and body, something taken for granted by all but
Navigius, who was convinced by a series of questions to which
he himself gave the right answers. Of the two components of
soul and body, the latter is nourished with food and thus grows
and becomes strong—but is there no food for the soul? Here
Monica intervened with a memorable response: "Obviously. I
believe that the soul is not nourished except by the understanding and knowledge of things."[54] Monica knew nothing
about Platonism or Aristotelianism, but with her mental acuity
she expressed the content of her experience in simple terms,
drawing from it a universal principle: a person experiences the
things around oneself, takes stock of them, discovers what they
have in common, formulates and verifies hypotheses, and
derives laws from them. In other words, one understands the
nature of things, as the Book of Genesis demonstrates (cf.
2:19–20) with the symbolic naming of the creatures, which
signifies the recognition of their natures. Monica meant that it
is through knowledge, or the understanding of things, that the
soul is nourished—in the sense that a person who grows in
knowledge grows in the spiritual dimension.

Trygetius manifested his doubts, and Monica explained
herself by saying:

> Did not you yourself today demonstrate from what and
> where the soul finds its nourishment? For, according to your
> own statement, you noticed only after a certain part of the
> breakfast which bowl we were using, since you had been
> thinking of some other things I do not know, although you
> helped yourself from that course and ate it. Where, then, was
> your mind at the time when it did not pay attention to what
> you were eating? From there, believe me, and by such meals
> is the soul nourished, that is, by those speculations and
> thoughts by which it is able to gain knowledge.[55]

Augustine tried to further clarify Monica's thought by making an observation that no one was able to refute: that the spirits of more highly cultivated persons are richer and more ample than those of the ignorant, which, in spiritual terms, we might call famished. Trygetius replied that the souls of the ignorant are also full, but they are full of vice and error. But these, Augustine responded, do not nourish the soul; rather they empty it. He then brought the conversation back under his direction:

> ...I think that on my birthday I ought to serve a somewhat richer meal, not only for our bodies, but also for our souls, since we all agree that man consists of two things: body and soul.... For, in case I tried to feed you against your will and taste, my undertaking would be in vain and prayers should be said that you would be more desirous for those meals than for the ones of the body. This will be the case if your souls are healthy, for sick souls, as can be seen in a diseased body, refuse their food and spit it out.[56]

This was Augustine's contention, and all declared in unison that they wanted to nourish their spirits.

The discussion then turned to the subject of happiness. The first assertion made was that the person who did not have what he or she desired could not be happy. Did that mean that anyone who possesses the object of one's desire is happy? Monica responded:

> If he wishes and possesses good things, he is happy; if he desires evil things—no matter if he possesses them—he is wretched.

Augustine smiled and responded:

> Mother, you have really gained the mastery of the very stronghold of philosophy. For, undoubtedly you were wanting the words to express yourself like Tullius, who also dealt with

this matter. In his *Hortensius*, a book written in the praise and defense of philosophy, he said: "Behold, not the philosophers, but only people who like to argue, state that all are happy who live according to their own will. This, of course, is not true, for, to wish what is not fitting is the worst of wretchedness. But is it not so deplorable to fail of attaining what we desire as it is to wish to attain what is not proper. For, greater evil is brought about through one's wicked will than happiness through fortune."[57]

Monica expressed her agreement with these words, and it seemed apparent to everyone that they had someone wise and profound in their midst. Augustine, meanwhile, tried to understand from what divine source Monica's thoughts sprang. Although she had never gone to school, her contact with God and her solid Christian formation had brought her to a wisdom that professional philosophers might envy.

The discussion continued by setting forth clearly that the good that one possesses in order to be happy must be eternal rather than transitory. In fact, those who desire fleeting things cannot be happy, because they might lose such intangible possessions. As a result, only God, who is the highest and eternal Good, can make people happy. But who is it that possesses God? Licentius maintained that it was the one who lives well. Trygetius and Lastidianus agreed that it was the one who does what God wants. Adeodatus said it was the one who does not have an unclean spirit, and his grandmother Monica immediately agreed with him.

Since the question was becoming too vast and difficult, they decided to take it up again the following day. For this spiritual banquet's "dessert," Augustine proceeded to take the conclusions the group had reached on the subject of happiness and apply them to the Academics. The Academics, he said, could never be happy, because they maintained that they could never reach the truth they desired. And since they could not be happy, neither were they wise, because true wisdom leads to happiness. Licentius, Trygetius, and Navigius, who understood a bit of philosophy, recognized what Augustine meant. But the others, who didn't know who the Academics were, remained outside of the conversation. So speaking for all of them, Monica asked her son to explain the Academics in a few words. After Augustine had done so, Monica came out with a quick-witted pun: "These men are *caducarii!*" (*Caducarii* was a common term for epileptics.) And the group adjourned amid the general good humor.

The next day the meeting began after lunch as always, and the discussion resumed with the three definitions of the possession of God that had already been given. The first two had the same meaning: living well is nothing else than doing the will of God. The third reply, given by Adeodatus, had to be analyzed in greater detail. For Adeodatus, not having an unclean spirit did not simply mean abstaining from the sins of the flesh but from every kind of sin. Abstaining from sin meant living well and doing the will of God. So in the final analysis, the three responses could be reduced to just one. And everyone agreed that this was so.

Again on this second day it was Monica who, in her wisdom, provided the decisive turning point in the discussion. Who has God within oneself? Is God not in everyone? How can the one who seeks God have God within? Monica answered all of these questions:

> He who lives righteously possesses God, that is, has Him propitious to him; he who lives a bad life also possesses God, but as hostile to him. But whoever is still seeking God, and has not yet found Him, has Him neither as propitious nor as hostile, yet is not without God.[58]

Only the third of these assertions was clarified during the discussion: the one who seeks God also has his favor, but only the one who has found him is happy. The one who is still seeking him, although he or she enjoys God's favor, is not yet happy.

On the third day the discussion turned to what unhappiness is. Monica had identified it as the lack of true wisdom. The group began to raise examples of people who, although they did not possess true wisdom, were very rich and therefore could not be called miserable. Then Monica said:

> I do not yet quite understand how misery can be separated from want, and want from misery. Although he had great riches and abundance and—according to your own statement—desired nothing more, he still was in want of wisdom, since he entertained the fear of losing these things. Are we going to consider him in want, if he be without silver and money, and not if he should lack wisdom?[59]

At these words, Augustine greatly rejoiced at his mother's philosophy; although she was illiterate, she had uttered the very words he had been waiting to pronounce at the end of their discussion as the summit of philosophical speculation. Addressing the entire group, he said:

> Do you all see now that a great difference exists between many and varied doctrines and a soul that is devoted to God? From what other source flow these words that we admire?[60]

The discussion continued with an exploration of the meaning of that true wisdom that is God himself and the only source of happiness. At one point Monica asked for the help of God on behalf of all, in order that they might attain this true wisdom. She prayed in the words of one of Ambrose's hymns, which had been engraved upon her mind through frequent repetition: *"Fove precantes, Trinitas!"* ("Help, O Trinity,

those that pray").[61] Again Monica had summed up in a few
words the entire conversation, exhorting all to attain that end
which is God, the true wisdom that makes us happy, walking
quickly toward him with solid faith, lively hope, and burning
charity. Thus ends the dialogue *On the Happy Life.*

In his *De Ordine* (On Order), Augustine again insisted that
his mother be present, since she had no other pressing business. He wrote that his long experience of life with her had
revealed to him her sharp intelligence and the burning of her
spirit for the things of God.[62] Moreover, the discussion of the
happy life had given him all the confirmation he needed of
Monica's philosophical bent, and he was genuinely proud of
her. For her part, with a combination of humility and humor,
Monica gently dismissed the fact that Augustine wanted to
have her questions written down, saying:

> "What is this you are doing? Have you ever read in your
> books that women have been permitted to participate in dis-
> cussions of this kind?" "I don't much care," Augustine replied,
> "about the opinions of the prideful and the ignorant, who
> read their books as casually as they greet people on the street.
> As a matter of fact, they pay no attention to who the people
> are that they greet, but to the clothes they wear and the airs
> they put on. When reading, they give no thought to the ori-
> gin of the question under consideration or the conclusions
> that the authors have decided upon ahead of time and their
> explanations and summaries. But since some of these are of
> no mean spirit (they are, in fact, tinged to some degree with
> learning and can easily be brought into the inner sanctum of
> philosophy), they were kept in consideration by our ancestors,
> and in the course of our correspondence I have seen that their
> books are also familiar to you. And to take just one example
> from our own times, a man who stands out for his intelli-
> gence, eloquence, and the blessings of fortune, Theodorus,[63]

whom you know well yourself, exerts himself so that no one either now or in the future will have any reason to complain of a lack of learning in our time. If someone, on the other hand, should pick up one of my books and, reading my name there, without saying 'Who is this?' and throwing the book away, either out of curiosity or excessive zeal should enter through the door in spite of its shoddy appearance, he will not find our discussions of philosophy tedious, nor perhaps will he scorn any of the thinkers who find a place in my reasonings. In fact, not only are they free, which is sufficient for any of the liberal arts and not only for philosophy, but their family origins are entirely respectable.

"The books of the most cultivated men speak also of shoemakers, and of even more humble kinds of persons, who have studied philosophy: and these have blazed with such a great light of intelligence and accomplishment that they would not have exchanged it for any other kind of nobility, even if they could have. And believe me, there will not be lacking a certain type of person who will find it more amusing that you speak of philosophy with me than if he found any other sort of silliness or gravity in my writings. In fact, women practiced philosophy in the ancient world, and besides, your philosophy pleases me greatly. In fact, mother, you should know that the Greek word 'philosophy' means 'love of wisdom.' For this reason, the divine scriptures, which you embrace with all your strength, do not command avoiding and despising the wise altogether, but only the wise of this world. There is another world far from our eyes, which is intuited by the minds of a few virtuous people, as Christ amply expresses. He does not say, 'My kingdom is not of *the* world,' but, 'My kingdom is not of *this* world.' In fact, those who think that all philosophy is to be avoided want nothing else than that we should not love wisdom. So I would be underestimating you in my book if you did not love wisdom; but I would not underestimate you if you loved it to a limited extent, and much less if you love it as much as I do. Now because you love wisdom much more than you love me, and I know very well how much you love me, and since you have made such great progress in it that you can no longer be intimidated by the fear of anything, not even death, something that is extremely difficult even for the wisest men, and all acknowledge that this is the highest summit of philosophy, why should not I myself wish to become your disciple?"[64]

At this point, Monica modestly and facetiously remarked that Augustine had never so exaggerated as he had that day.

There are also moments during these dialogues when Augustine praises his mother's wisdom and philosophical attitude. Although she did not have the tools of the trade, such as various historical and technical methods, her spirit was mature and keen. She was detached from her passions, and she intuited the truth more easily than those who knew the techniques of speculation but were made spiritually sluggish by their desires. Monica's way of speaking was not without its defects of form and expression. The Italians criticized Augustine for his pronunciation, and he, in turn, criticized others for similar defects. But these are petty concerns, and Monica rightly disdained them. They deal with the body of learning, but Monica had mastered its spirit. The important thing, which Monica did, is to hold firm to faith and to Sacred Scripture, and Augustine exhorted her to maintain these habits.

Monica demonstrated her agility in reasoning through conversations recounted in other passages of De Ordine, such as when she spoke of the justice of God, which consists in judging between good and evil and giving each what he or she deserves. She also explained the origin of evil, which does not come from God but is a distortion of the order that God intends.[65]

A much clearer view of Monica's character emerges from the ideas and beliefs expressed during the conversations at Cassiciacum. She was not a small-minded, nitpicking woman who tried to stand apart by despising the world and always having a criticism ready. The tears she had wept in prayer were the tears of a strong and sensitive woman. Cassiciacum also reveals her sense of humor. She carried herself with simplicity during the discussions, never acting like a know-it-all, yet she had the ability to make concepts clearer and more approachable. Her quips show that she was witty and fun to be with, confirming that her holiness was not some long-faced, heavy affair. It was comprised instead of an interior solidity, a spiritual richness, a depth of intuition and feeling combined with a serenity that came from her contact with God and that expressed itself in her humble, courteous, and agreeable behavior.

In the dialogues one also discovers Monica's desire to always improve herself and learn new things. She did not consider her fifty-five years of age an obstacle or impediment. She sat on the lawn fully engaged, participating freely in the discussions held by this group of ardent young men. Knowing both how to listen and how to speak her mind, she could integrate a variety of ideas and reach precise conclusions. So it was no exaggeration for Augustine to refer to her as a philosopher and even to state that she had reached the pinnacle of philosophy.

The mark of a youthful spirit is the desire to learn and discover new things, without ever becoming too comfortable with one's extent of knowledge. With her open and youthful spirit, her mental sharpness and capacity to reach profound and interesting conclusions, Monica demonstrated the work that God had accomplished in her by combining supernatural

wisdom and human intelligence. This is something not granted to proud, self-absorbed persons, who remain desperately
closed within their own misery. Jesus, in fact, said: "I thank
you, Father, Lord of heaven and earth, because you have hid-
den these things from the wise and the intelligent and have
revealed them to infants" (Mt 11:25).

St. Catherine of Siena, who was illiterate, and St. Thérèse of
Lisieux, a humble Carmelite who died at the age of twenty-
four, were both proclaimed Doctors of the Church. They
confirm the fact that the gift of divine wisdom flourishing in
a pure spirit reveals far more than does human reason nourished by its own efforts. In the thoughts and writings of the
saints, as exemplified by St. Monica, one finds greater depth
and intuition than in the most famous philosophers and the-
ologians.

CHAPTER XII

The Great Triumph

For Monica, Augustine, and the other members of the group, the six months in Cassiciacum were a sort of prolonged spiritual retreat. They had not come together merely for philosophical investigation, which, when it is conducted with a pure spirit, cannot help but lead to God. They also read the Scriptures, prayed, recited the psalms, and sang hymns under Monica's guidance. They could not have had better preparation for baptism. Augustine's catechumenate had lasted since his birth, and now, through a definitive and solemn act of the will, he would put into practice everything that had been growing within his spirit during that long journey.

In the fourth century, baptism was celebrated at the Easter Vigil, the mother of all vigils, the night on which Christians gathered to await the dawn of the first day of the week—Sunday, a day made glorious by the resurrection of Christ. On that night, together with Christ, catechumens died to the old

life, the life of sin, and rose again with Christ to live a new life.
Baptism was their Passover, the passage from the old to the
new.

Augustine and his friends had certainly become new men.
They left Cassiciacum with extraordinary fervor and with a
firm commitment to consecrate their lives to God and to the
Church, to truth and goodness. The trip from Cassiciacum to
Milan was a pious pilgrimage. Alypius, with the zeal of a neophyte, wanted to go barefoot even though the roads were still
frozen over. They needed to reach Ambrose's city by the
beginning of Lent, which fell on March 10 that year, in order
to be entered among the "eligible" or "elect," those who
would receive baptism at the next Easter Vigil.

The last Lent before baptism was the most intense period
of the catechumenate. Daily instructions were given. Meanwhile, the candidates underwent certain preparatory rites,
such as the exorcism of the catechumen and the handing over
and handing back of symbols—that is, the memorization and
public profession of the articles of Christian faith.

One can imagine how Monica's heart rejoiced during
these days of anticipation. Her prayer must have intensified, as
she interceded with the Lord to ask that the work he had
begun in her son now come to a happy conclusion.

With great humility, Augustine, together with Alypius and
his son, Adeodatus, blended into the crowd of catechumens
from Milan who were also preparing for baptism. He listened
to the words of Ambrose and joined in singing the liturgical
hymns, which, as he would later acknowledge, moved him to
tears and filled his heart with an agreeable sweetness and a
sense of being lifted up to the Lord.

Monica's discreet presence at his side was no longer characterized by anxiety but by a deep and overpowering joy. In

the time not absorbed by his commitments as a catechumen, Augustine no longer sought diversions or distractions but continued immersing himself in meditation. The results of this can be seen in some of his writings during those days, like *De Immortalitate Animae* (On the Immortality of the Soul) and *De Musica* (On Music).

During Holy Week, his concentration became even more focused, and he thought constantly of baptism. Together with the assembly of the faithful, Monica followed the last phases of the catechumenate and the rites of preparation for the sacrament.

Her exultation reached its peak on the night of Holy Saturday. During the ceremony, Ambrose touched the ears of her son Augustine, her grandson, Adeodatus, and Alypius, and said to them, "*Ephphatha,*" meaning "be opened" (that is, be open to hearing the message of God, so that you may proclaim it with your mouth). Her son then proclaimed his solemn commitment to renounce the devil and turn toward the east in order to go to meet Christ. The catechumens listened to the passages from Scripture that tell the Easter story, and they sang more with their heart than their lips the words of Psalm 42: "As a deer longs for flowing streams, so my soul longs for you, O God!" Finally the great moment came for Augustine to descend into the regenerating waters and emerge as a new creature in the profession of the true faith he had once opposed. Now he was preparing to glorify and defend the faith with the depth of his mind and the holiness of his life. His head was anointed with the holy chrism oil, signifying the royal priesthood that he had received by being incorporated into Christ, in his Mystical Body, which is the Church. Augustine then put on the white garment that would allow him to participate in the banquet of the Kingdom of heaven. Monica would now be able for the first time to participate with him in the sacred mysteries, to draw near to the same table together with him to eat the same bread and drink the same wine.[66] What else could life possibly hold in store? What more could she desire? The dream she had held onto over so many years—through penance, fasting, and tears—had now come true before her very eyes.

The Lord had heard his faithful servant, and nothing remained for her now but holy rejoicing. The son to whom she had given birth amid the pains of labor, she had now brought to a new birth—this time also amid suffering—to the life that does not pass away. This holy night—the night between April 24 and 25 of 387—was Monica's triumph.

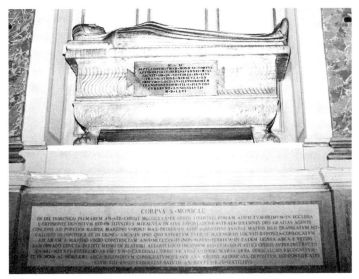

A statue of Monica lying in state by Isaia da Pisa, fifteenth century, on the tomb in the chapel of St. Monica in the Church of St. Augustine, Rome.

The sepulcher of 1760, with the body of St. Monica, placed beneath the altar of the chapel of St. Monica in the Church of St. Augustine.

The entrance of the parish Church of St. Monica in Ostia Lido, Rome, inaugurated on December 7, 1972.

The interior of the Church of St. Monica.

The Basilica of Santa Aurea (fifteenth century) in Ostia Antica.
To the left is the entrance for the ancient residence of the bishop of Ostia.

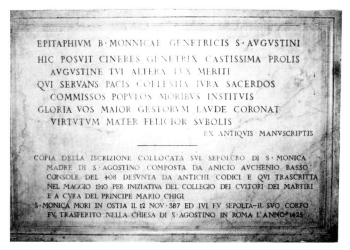

EPITAPHIVM B·MONNICAE GENETRICIS S·AVGVSTINI
HIC POSVIT CINERES GENETRIX CASTISSIMA PROLIS
    AVGVSTINE TVI ALTERA LVX MERITI
QVI SERVANS PACIS COELESTIA IVRA SACERDOS
    COMMISSOS POPVLOS MORIBVS INSTITVIS
GLORIA VOS MAIOR GESTORVM LAVDE CORONAT
VIRTVTVM MATER FELICIOR SVBOLIS
                    EX ANTIQVIS MANVSCRIPTIS

COPIA DELLA ISCRIZIONE COLLOCATA SVL SEPOLCRO DI S·MONICA
MADRE DI S·AGOSTINO COMPOSTA DA ANICIO AVCHENIO BASSO
CONSOLE DEL 408 DESVNTA DA ANTICHI CODICI E QVI TRASCRITTA
NEL MAGGIO 1910 PER INIZIATIVA DEL COLLEGIO DEI CVLTORI DEI MARTIRI
E A CVRA DEL PRINCIPE MARIO CHIGI
S·MONICA MORI IN OSTIA IL 12 NOV·387 ED IVI FV SEPOLTA–IL SVO CORPO
FV TRASFERITO NELLA CHIESA DI S·AGOSTINO IN ROMA L'ANNO 1425

In the Basilica of Santa Aurea is found this marble slab with a copy of the
epitaph Auchenius Bassus had engraved on the sepulcher of St. Monica.

The Church of St. Augustine in Campo Marzio in Rome,
built by Cardinal Guillaume d'Estouteville in 1483.

CHAPTER XIII

Ostia on the Tiber

Augustine's philosophical circle in Milan was already evolving into a small monastic family. But what were they still doing in Milan? It was not their homeland. Augustine had come there to teach, and his mother, his brother, and his friends had joined him. Milan was the city Providence had chosen so that Augustine's conversion might come to fruition through the work of Ambrose. But now there was no longer any reason for them to stay. Augustine had left his teaching post. The city was too noisy for the kind of life he intended to lead, and money was beginning to run short. To all of this were added rumors of war and subversion. Ambrose himself had gone to Treviri to meet with the usurper Maximus to persuade him to accept peace.

Various factors influenced the group to return to their own land of Africa, including the fact that they owned some property there. The place naturally had a hold on their hearts.

They decided to return to Tagaste, where they would realize their dream of a philosophical and monastic community.

They left Milan for Rome. From the port city of Ostia (which literally means "the gates" of Rome) they would depart for Africa as soon as possible.

It was probably May of 387. Spring was making itself felt in the mild weather, the greening of the trees, and the scent of flowers. Although the voyage would inevitably involve some discomfort, the reawakening of nature lightened their thoughts considerably.

Monica began the trip back with a completely different attitude than the one she had on her first voyage. Now she simply wanted to enjoy her time with Augustine. For his part, Augustine foresaw that her end was not far off, and so he tried to spend as much time with her as possible.

Adeodatus, who was fourteen years old, was another of Monica's consolations. In his writings, Augustine draws a portrait of the boy that is full of admiration. Although he was still very young, Adeodatus surpassed many learned and seasoned men in intelligence. This was certainly due to the gift of God; Augustine confessed that he had contributed nothing other than his sin in begetting him.[67]

But Monica had seen to the young man's education and obtained better and more immediate results with him than she had with Augustine. The reply Adeodatus gave in Cassiciacum, that the person with a pure soul possesses God, echoed Monica's teaching about the happiness reserved to the pure of heart. Later Adeodatus would also be one of the characters in the dialogue *The Teacher,* which Augustine composed in Tagaste when his son was sixteen years old. His intelligence was exceptional in every area, and gave promise for the future. This intelligence, furthermore, was combined with innocence and virtue. Adeodatus's premature death at the age of eighteen has deprived history of seeing what he might have become. One can imagine Monica's great love for him and the immense happiness his presence brought her.

⟨⟩

The group arrived at Ostia on the Tiber. The sea was almost two miles closer to Rome then than it is today, extending to the place where the well-preserved remnants of the port— with its houses, forum, and theater—mark the site of Ostia Antica. The ground gained by the land in its battle against the sea is currently the site of modern-day Ostia, a rapidly expanding suburb of Rome. In 1956, a parish was built in this city in honor of St. Monica. The large, modern-style church was finished in 1972. It does not contain any relics of the saint but only a wooden statue given and blessed by Pius XII, intended as a fitting commemoration and homage to one who ended her earthly journey at that spot sixteen centuries earlier.

The historic city of Ostia, which was then located at the mouth of the Tiber, dominated the sea in its day. Monica, Augustine, and the others found lodging at one of the homes of Ostia, and there, far from the noise of the capital, they rested in peace for a few days after the exertion of their journey. Unfortunately, the exact location of the house that had the fortune of welcoming this band of saints is not known. It was probably like so many others that have left nothing but scant ruins for visitors to admire. Within the enclosure of the house was a garden with a window looking out onto it.

One evening at sunset, Monica and Augustine were alone together looking out the window at the countryside. Their conversation did not revolve around frivolous topics; they had forgotten the past and were entirely focused on the future. The marvelous, if romanticized, painting by Ary Scheffer depicts the scene, with a young Augustine dressed in a toga and seated like a teacher, gazing far into the distance. He has the look of one absorbed in contemplation, his head propped up by his right hand and his left hand in those of Monica. She is seated above him, with her head tilted upward and her eyes fixed upon heaven in an expression of mystical exaltation.

Monica no longer thought of anything but heaven. What would the eternal life of the saints be like? Mother and son considered what the marvels of that future life would be—she with her intuition and he with his profound intellect. Augustine recounts:

> Our colloquy led us to the point where the pleasures of the body's senses, however intense and in however brilliant a material light enjoyed, seemed unworthy not merely of comparison but even of remembrance beside the joy of that life, and we lifted ourselves in longing yet more ardent toward *That Which Is,* and step by step traversed all bodily creatures and heaven iteslf, whence sun and moon and stars shed their light upon the earth. Higher still we mounted by inward thought and wondering discource on your works, and we arrived at the summit of our own minds; and this too we transcended, to touch that land of never-failing plenty where you pasture Israel for ever with the food of truth. Life there is in the Widsom through whom all things are made, and all others that have been or ever will be; but Wisdom herself is not made: she is as she always has been and will be for ever. Rather should we say that in her there is no "has been" or "will be," but only being, for she is eternal, but past and future do not belong to eternity. And as we talked and panted for it, we just touched the edge of it by the utmost leap of our

hearts; then, sighing and unsatisfied, we left the first-fruits of
our spirit captive there, and returned to the noise of articulate
speech, where a word has beginning and end. How different
from your Word, our Lord, who abides in himself, and grows
not old, but renews all things.

Then we said,
"If the tumult of the flesh fell silent for someone,
and silent too were the phantasms of earth, sea and air,
silent the heavens,
and the very soul silent to itself,
that it might pass beyond itself by not thinking of its own
        being;
if dreams and revelations known through its imagination
        were silent,
if every tongue, and every sign, and whatever is subject to
        transience were wholly stilled for him
—for if anyone listens, all these things will tell him,
'We did not make ourselves;
he made us who abides for ever'—
and having said this they held their peace
for they had pricked the listening ear to him who made
        them;
and then he alone were to speak,
not through things that are made, but of himself,
that we might hear his Word,
not through fleshly tongue nor angel's voice,
nor thundercloud,
nor any riddling parable,
hear him unmediated, whom we love in all these things,
hear him without them,
as now we stretch out and in a flash of thought
touch that eternal Wisdom who abides above all things;
if this could last,
and all other visions, so far inferior, be taken away,
and this sight alone ravish him who saw it,

and engulf him and hide him away, kept for inward joys,
so that this moment of knowledge—
this passing moment that left us aching for more—
should there be life eternal,
would not *Enter into the joy of your Lord*
be this, and this alone?
And when, when will this be?
When we all rise again, but not all are changed?"[68]

This famous passage from Augustine recounts the extraordinary event that would be immortalized as the ecstasy at Ostia. For one moment, the Lord permitted Monica and Augustine to contemplate, beyond the boundaries of time, the eternal happiness that comes from God himself. Beginning with earthly things that bear the mark of their Creator, mother and son rose up higher and higher, bringing all created things to silence, coming into direct contact with God.

This episode belongs to the realm of mystical phenomena experienced by saints throughout history, although such experiences are rare. These visions and intuitions cannot be expressed in human words, as St. Paul says:

I know a person in Christ who fourteen years ago was caught up to the third heaven—whether in the body or out of the body I do not know; God knows. And I know that this person—whether in the body or out of the body I do not know; God knows—was caught up into paradise and heard things that are not to be told, that no mortal is permitted to repeat (2 Cor 12:2–4).

Thus St. Monica belongs to the rank of the mystics, which is not a category restricted to persons living the contemplative religious life. Monica, a wife and mother leading a fully active life and immersed in the realities of her world, teaches us that the highest form of prayer, which is contemplation, is the prerogative of all Christians. God, for his part, gives gifts as he wishes. And yet one does not reach this state of prayer suddenly or by accident. In this particular vision of the eternal happiness that is the ultimate meaning of human existence, Monica, who had come to the end of her earthly journey, was reaping the reward of a life of union with God, in the midst of a full range of material concerns.

For Augustine, this was an unforgettable experience he would always carry in his heart, an interior reminder that would drive him from that point on to give himself body and soul to the things of God. For Monica, it was a foretaste of paradise. After this intuition, fleeting as it was, she became indifferent to the visible world, and its pleasures no longer held any appeal. As Monica said to her son:

> For my part, my son, I find pleasure no longer in anything this life holds. What I am doing here still, or why I tarry, I do not know, for all worldly hope has withered away for me. One thing only there was for which I desired to linger awhile in this life: to see you a Catholic Christian before I died. And this my God has granted to me more lavishly than I could have hoped, letting me see you even spurning earthly happiness to be his servant. What now keeps me here?[69]

Augustine was so caught up in ecstasy that his mind was elsewhere. While his mother was saying these things he could barely follow them, nor could he remember later what he said to her in reply.

Now both of them saw things from a different perspective, from God's point of view. From this vantage point, Augustine understood that he had before him a long and important mission to which he could dedicate his youthful energy. Monica, on the other hand, had faithfully carried out the mission entrusted to her and was simply awaiting the reward of the just.

Chapter XIV

Death and Burial

Summer had begun, and the African friends were still preparing to take advantage of the favorable season and sail for Carthage. But other events would intervene.

A little more than five days after her mystical experience, Monica became seriously ill and was confined to bed. The departure was delayed, and soon all the young men began to gather around her sickbed, seeking to alleviate her sufferings and hoping for her healing. Her fever climbed, and Monica slipped into delirium. Everyone grew anxious, especially Augustine, Navigius, and Monica's sensitive grandson, Adeodatus.

At one point Monica became lucid. Seeing everyone gathered about her bed and not realizing what had happened, she asked in confusion, "Where was I?" No one replied; they were speechless with bewilderment and sorrow. Then Monica, realizing that the end was near, said in a quiet voice, "Here you will bury your mother."

Augustine was too choked to speak. Navigius made an effort to encourage Monica, telling her that the end had not yet come, that they would return to their homeland and she would finish her days in the land of her birth. But at these words, Monica gave him a reproachful look. He was still too bound by earthly concerns, preoccupied with things she had long left behind. She looked for confirmation of this in Augustine's face; he had shared that moment of mystical ecstasy with her and was closer than ever to her way of thinking. She said to him, "What silly talk!" Then, making a supreme effort to gather her strength in order to speak clearly, she said, "Lay this body anywhere, and take no trouble over it. One thing only do I ask of you, that you remember me at the altar of the Lord wherever you may be."[70]

She then fell silent and her breathing became shallow. Her illness was gaining the upper hand. Monica continued to suffer greatly, but she spoke no more; the words she had just pronounced remained the compendium of her faith and her testament for her children. Having reached the heights of sanctity, she no longer thought of earthly affairs, not even the most legitimate objects of concern, such as her own burial. She was interested only in her eternal destiny. The way in which her children would really be able to help her would be through prayer, and especially through the Eucharistic sacrifice.

Even so, Augustine remembered the great care with which Monica had prepared Patricius's tomb after his death. She had made plans for her body to be laid to rest alongside his, since they wanted to be united in the memory of their descendants just as they had been united on earth. Sixteen years had passed since then. Monica had run quickly along the way of perfection, and she had been refined by the Lord's grace. Now she was ready to rise above such physical concerns, having attained a purely spiritual view of them.

Augustine recalled hearing some people in Ostia say that Monica had spoken to them of this life with disdain and of death as good. They had said to her: "Dying may be all right ...but what about dying far from your country?" For the ancients, in fact, dying in exile and being buried where no one would ever return to honor your body was the greatest misfortune imaginable. Yet Monica, with her deeply Christian sentiments, had responded, "Nothing is far from God....There is no danger that at the end of the world he will not know where to find me and raise me up."[71] She was using her usual wit to affirm a profound truth.

The breviaries of the Augustinian Order imaginatively recount Monica's last days and include quaint stories about her. They relate that it was impossible for her to receive the Eucharist because of her stomach pains, and tell the story of a child who entered her room and then vanished. Such legendary episodes have even been immortalized in art. But perhaps it is more historically accurate to imagine the scene of her passing with the sober and brisk description that Augustine employs in the *Confessions.*[72]

Monica suffered from a violent fever for nine days. Pain can be an instrument of purification, a means of uniting oneself more intimately with the suffering of Christ. In her conscious moments, did she perhaps raise her spirit to God and offer her illness to him? Just days before, she had been privileged to enjoy a mystical vision of heaven. It's not unrealistic to picture her in her lucid moments desiring to pass from this fleeting earthly life to that homeland where "death [would] be no more; mourning and crying and pain [would] be no more" (cf. Rev 21:4).

She suffered intensely, and her desire for union with her Lord grew in proportion. Surrounded at the end by those who loved her, almost imperceptibly, she peacefully breathed her last. For Monica, the sacred moment of death meant passing from time into eternity. At that instant, in the light of God who judges, she entered into the fullness of the truth and saw her entire life, from her birth until her last moment, enfolded in the love of God. With exultation she clung to God, who is Truth, Love, Beauty, and the joy of his saints.

When she died, Monica was fifty-six years old and Augustine was thirty-three. The year was 387, and it was probably summertime.[73]

Though Augustine had known that his mother was dying, when she drew her last breath he realized the magnitude of his loss. He would never again see her face upon this earth, never again hear her voice. He knew that he owed everything he was to his mother. Tears threatened, but he submerged his grief in the depths of his soul, imposing strict control over his feelings. He suffered tremendous torment as he stood there rigidly, fighting between the pain moving him to weep and his self-control, which would not permit the tears to escape. Adeodatus, however, could not keep such tight reign over his emotions; he expressed his tender love for his grandmother and the overwhelming loss he felt with heavy weeping and loud sobs. A few of the people standing nearby took hold of him and led him out of his grandmother's room.

It was the reassurance of faith that gave them the strength to accept Monica's death. They were convinced that Monica had not died a miserable death, that she was not even dead at all—and this conviction sprang from Monica's own teaching and from her upright life, which certainly had earned for her eternal happiness.

Their sorrow was the painful wound caused by sudden separation after such a sweet and precious life together. Augustine found comfort in the words his mother had spoken to him during her final illness. She had responded to the kindness and duty he had shown her by telling him that he was pious and by recalling fondly that she had never received a harsh or offensive word from him. Because of the honor Augustine had always paid his mother, as well as the constant support and service she had given to him throughout his life, he was devastated by Monica's death. It was as if his life had been torn apart, as if a part of himself had been cut away. After all, his life and the life of his mother had become one.

Choking back sobs, Augustine's friend Evodius, who intended to begin the monastic life with him in Tagaste, took up the psalter and began to sing Psalm 100, while everyone else in the house sang the refrain: "I will sing the mercy and the justice of the Lord." Hearing the singing, the neighbors realized what had happened and began to fill the room where Monica's lifeless body lay. They were mostly fellow Christians who had observed with admiration the fervor of these new African converts and had struck up a close friendship with them during their stay in Ostia. Certain pious Christian women also came to unite with them in prayer. They tried to comfort Augustine and his brother with the usual things that are said in such circumstances. They stood in a room apart, soothing one another while the persons responsible for preparing funerals went about their tasks. To those persons it seemed—because of the self-control he had imposed on himself—that Augustine felt no sorrow. But the Lord knew the torment he suffered. He bore two sorrows: the natural pain of his mother's death, and the pain of feeling this sorrow when he should have been rejoicing because of his mother's good fortune, which in his Christian faith he believed in firmly. For this reason, just when he was about to break down he would restrain himself from crying, making an effort to keep his face expressionless. He accompanied his mother's body as it was carried to burial without shedding a tear.

It was customary to celebrate the Mass for the deceased while the body lay near the tomb, before placing it inside. Augustine did not even cry during the prayers that were recited at the Mass. He outwardly restrained himself while the grief pierced him deeply within. He tried to lessen his anguish by later taking a bath (Augustine followed the opinion that the Greek word for bath, *balanion,* meant "relaxation"), but when he came out nothing had changed. He went to sleep; when he woke up his pain had subsided somewhat, but then the thought of his mother immediately came to mind. He recalled her holy life and everything she had done for him. He could no longer hold back his tears. He let them come flooding from his heart, tears for his mother and for himself. Augustine wept in the sight of the Lord, away from indiscreet eyes and ears that might have assigned an unkind and insensitive interpretation to his sorrow. He concludes his narrative of this event in the *Confessions* by saying:

> Let anyone read it who will, and judge it as he will, and if he finds it sinful that I wept over my mother for a brief part of a single hour—the mother who for a little space was to my sight dead, and who had wept long years for me that in your sight I might live—then let such a reader not mock, but rather, if his charity is wide enough, himself weep for my sins to you, who are Father to all whom your Christ calls his brethren.[74]

It is also worth looking at the prayer that Augustine raised to God on behalf of his mother thirteen years after her death:

But now that my heart is healed of that wound, in which I was perhaps guilty of some carnal affection, I pour out to you tears of a very different kind for this servant of yours, O our God; they come gushing forth from a mind struck by the perils besetting every soul that dies in Adam. True, she had been brought to new life in Christ, and even before her release from the body she so lived that her faith and conduct redounded to the glory of your name. Yet all the same I dare not assert that from the time you brought her new birth in baptism no word contrary to your commandment escaped her lips. And by the Truth who is your Son we are warned, *If anyone says to his brother, "You fool!" he will be liable to hellfire,* so woe betide anyone, even one whose life is praiseworthy, if you should examine it without mercy! But since you are not ruthless in searching out our faults, we trustingly hope for a place in your house. If anyone were to give you an account of his real merits, what else would that be but a list of your gifts? If only humans would acknowledge that they are human, and anyone minded to boast would boast in the Lord!

This is why, O God of my heart, my praise, my life, I will for a little while disregard her good deeds, for which I joyfully give you thanks, and pray to you now for my mother's sins. Hear me through that healing remedy who hung upon the tree, the medicine for our wounds who sits at your right hand and intercedes for us. I know that she dealt mercifully with others and from her heart forgave her debtors their debts; do you then forgive her any debts she contracted during all those years after she had passed through the saving waters. Forgive her, Lord, forgive, I beg you, and do not arraign her before you. Let mercy triumph over judgment, for you, whose utterances are true, have to the merciful promised mercy. Since their very power to be merciful was your gift to them in the first place, you will be showing mercy to those with whom you have yourself dealt mercifully, and granting pity to those toward whom you have shown pity first.

I believe you have already done what I am asking you, but look favorably, Lord, on this free offering of my lips. On the day when her release was at hand she gave no thought to costly burial or the embalming of her body with spices, nor did she pine for a special monument or concern herself about a grave in her native land; no, that was not her command to us. She desired only to be remembered at your altar, where she had served you with never a day's absence. From that altar, as she knew, the holy Victim is made available to us, he through whom the record of debt that stood against us was annulled. He has triumphed over an enemy who does keep a tally of our faults and looks for anything to lay to our charge, but finds no case against him. In him we win our victory. Who will reimburse him for that innocent blood? Who will pay back to him the price he paid to purchase us, as though to snatch us back from him?

To the sacrament of that ransom-price your handmaid made fast her soul with the bonds of faith. Let no one wrench her away from your protection. Let no lion or dragon thrust in between by force or guile; for she will not claim that she has no debts to pay, lest she be convicted by the crafty accuser and fall into his power; she will reply only that her debts have been forgiven by him to whom no one can repay what he paid for us, though he owed us nothing.

May she then rest in peace with her husband. She was married to no other man either before or after him, and in serving him she brought forth fruit for you by patience, to win him for you in the end. Inspire others, my Lord, my God, inspire your servants who are my brethren, your children who are my masters, whom I now serve with heart and voice and pen, that as many of them as read this may remember Monica, your servant, at your altar, along with Patricius, sometime her husband. From their flesh you brought me into this life, though how I do not know. Let them remember with loving devotion these two who were my parents in this transitory light, but also were my brethren under you, our Father, within our mother the Catholic Church, and my fellow-citizens in the eternal Jerusalem, for which your people sighs with longing throughout its pilgrimage, from its setting out to its return. So may the last request she made of me be granted to her more abundantly by the prayers of many, evoked by my confessions, than by my prayers alone.[75]

Augustine concludes the ninth book of the *Confessions,* largely dedicated to his mother, with these moving words. He was convinced that his only way of communicating with her was through the Lord, through prayer. He does not hesitate to assert that if they could communicate in some other way, his mother would be close to him at every moment:

> If the souls of the dead took part in the affairs of the living, and if it were their very selves that, when we see them, speak to us in sleep; to say nothing of others, there is my own self, whom my pious mother would no night fail to visit, that mother who by land and sea followed me that she might live with me. Far be the thought that she should, by a life more happy, have been made cruel, to that degree that when any thing vexes my heart she should not even console in his sadness the son whom she loved with an only love, whom she never wished to see mournful.[76]

In the work from which the preceding quotation was taken—*De Cura pro Mortuis Gerenda* (On the Care of the Dead)—Augustine writes of the significance of Christian burial as an honor bestowed on the body, which was the instrument of the soul in doing good, and as an incentive for prayer on behalf of the deceased. For this reason, although Augustine certainly believed that the prayers of suffrage for the dead were more important, we cannot imagine that he would have completely ignored his mother's burial.

Among the ancients, the remains of the dead were either cremated or buried. To demonstrate their faith in the resurrection, Christians eliminated the practice of cremation, and during the period of the catacombs they used burial niches. When they emerged from the catacombs, they began to use caskets, more or less elaborate. Monica was enclosed in one of these and placed among the tombs in the cemetery of Ostia.

Augustine frequently came to pray at his mother's tomb during the year he remained in Rome before returning to Africa in 388. He was ordained a priest in 391, consecrated bishop in 396, and died in 430. In all that time he did not return to Rome, so he never saw that hallowed tomb again. But it certainly must have been visited and cared for by his friends, who came to Rome from time to time to attend to business.

Augustine was still alive at the beginning of the fifth century, and the former consul Anicius Auchenius Bassus wanted to honor him by having six lines of elegiac poetry inscribed on Monica's tomb. The Latin inscription is translated as follows:

Here lies the chaste mother of a great son;
O Augustine, the star of the favor you won.
As priest you bring heaven's peace and light
To your people. Your praise and hers is great,
But on both a greater glory has smiled:
She who loved virtue exults in her child.

These verses, transcribed by a pilgrim before the tomb was forgotten, are found in twelve texts that date back to the eighth century and after. The existence of this epitaph was asserted in the *Hispana Collectio,* also called the "Isidorian Collection" because it was erroneously attributed to Isidore of Seville. The collection began to take shape during the fifth century; it relates the proceedings of the councils in its first section and pontifical decrees in the second.

In 1946, the famous Augustinian patristic scholar Antonio Casamassa found a longitudinal section of the burial chamber's stone containing a little more than a third of the inscription. This was placed in one of the side chapels of the Church of Santa Aurea in Ostia Antica.

Chapter XV

Beyond Death

Monica's life and virtues, which Augustine illustrates with affection and consummate artistry, immediately began to fascinate Christian readers. His depiction of Monica was not the conventional story of sanctity usually imaged as consecration to God in the religious life. Here, instead, was a mother like so many others, who had had to face difficulties that are common to many women: difficult relationships with their husbands and anxiety for the future of their children. Monica had become holy not by leaving the world behind but by giving an example of how Christians should live their married lives, establishing a proper hierarchy of values and relating everything to the Lord.

Despite interest in her life, however, an official movement of devotion to St. Monica did not develop until the beginning of the twelfth century. A certain priest named Walter, a canon regular* from the town of Arrouaise in France, maintained that he had made arrangements for the transfer of St. Monica's relics to his monastery in 1162. Interestingly, although no credence was given to Walter's claims, this is precisely the year in which the feast of St. Monica began to be celebrated—on May 4, believed to be the vigil of St. Augustine's conversion.

It was commonly held that Monica's remains could be found in the Church of Santa Aurea, where they had been moved during the sixth or seventh century in order to better preserve them. Pope Martin V saw God's providence at work in St. Monica's death and burial in Ostia. In Africa, her remains probably would have been scattered by the invasion of the barbarian Vandals in the fifth century.

Devotion to St. Monica was extended to the universal Church in 1430, the year her relics were located and transferred at Pope Martin's behest. That year also marked the beginnings of iconography devoted to St. Monica. The cycle of frescoes that Benozzo Gozzoli later painted in the choir loft of the church dedicated to St. Augustine in San Gimignano, Tuscany, is particularly worth noting. These frescoes, painted between 1463 and 1465, feature St. Monica in various scenes from Augustine's life.

In 1430, Pope Martin V had created a small commission of Augustinian hermits headed by the bishop of Aleth. The commission was charged with investigating the area around the Church of Santa Aurea in the hope of discovering St. Monica's remains. Excavations began under the altar of Santa Aurea, partly on the basis of advice from inhabitants of the area, who had preserved an oral tradition that the saint's remains were located there. At first the excavations revealed nothing of particular interest, but then workers discovered a small opening

---

* A member of a religious institute of regular priests living in community under the Augustinian Rule. —Ed.

that permitted access to a deeper subterranean area. There they found six tombs, three on one side and three on the other, with names inscribed upon them. The three on the right contained the remains of three popes: Linus, Felix, and Anterus. The three on the left were the tombs of Constantia, Aurea, and Monica.

The commissioners placed the remains in a wooden box and took them to Rome. News of what was happening spread, and a great crowd began to gather. The next day, the pontiff ordered that a marble casket be brought to Rome. The transfer of the relics took place on Palm Sunday, April 9, 1430, as authenticated by the letter from Martin V, *Pia Caritas,* dated April 27, 1430, and by Maffeo Vegio's *Translationis Ordo.* Vegio was a famous man of letters of the time.[77]

A well-known speech on the occasion of the transfer was attributed to Martin V, but Augustinian Father Antonio Casamassa[78] has shown that it was actually composed by another Augustinian, Father Andrea Biglia. Apart from praising St. Monica, who is considered a mother more in the spiritual than in the physical sense, the speech relates the various miracles said to have taken place through contact with the venerated relics: the healing of children brought forward by their mothers and the restoration of sight to the blind. These miracles seem to express symbolically Monica's earthly mission to bring her son to spiritual healing and recovery of sight, a mission that now continues through her intercession with God in the Kingdom of heaven.

The relics were temporarily placed in the Church of San Trifone. A few years later, Benedictine Cardinal Guillaume d'Estouteville (1403–1483), the bishop of Rouen, dispensed his wealth to the Church of St. Augustine, Rome, so that St. Monica's remains could be preserved in a worthy manner.

They are there to this day, under the altar of a chapel decorated with frescoes depicting stories from the life of St. Monica. Her remains were transferred there from an earlier casket that incorporated a statue of Monica lying in state, which had been created by Isaia da Pisa during the fifteenth century. In 1566, a Latin inscription was carved onto the casket. It reads:

> Jesus Christ. The sepulcher in which the body of blessed Monica lay, in Ostia on the Tiber, for one thousand and forty years. On account of the miracles that took place during the transfer of her relics, her most devoted children provided that her remains be moved from their obscure place of rest to a more visible one, in the year of salvation 1566.

Beneath the casket another inscription in Latin provides a summary of the various transfers of St. Monica's body until its present location, under the altar of the chapel dedicated to St. Monica in the Church of St. Augustine in Campo Marzio. This last transfer took place during the pontificate of Clement XIII, on August 1, 1760. The altar itself was consecrated by an Augustinian, Bishop Giuseppe Maria Castellani of Porfireone, Italy, on December 18, 1851.

The inscription is translated as follows:

> The body of St. Monica, brought out of Ostia on the Tiber on Palm Sunday in the year 1430 of the Christian era, was first deposited in the Church of San Trifone, while the Supreme Pontiff Martin V solemnly addressed the people, giving thanks to God for the singular miracles that had taken place during its transfer. Then, during the pontificate of Callistus III, it was transferred to the Church of St. Augustine, the son of this great woman, and was placed near the altar built by Maffeo Vegio, in a wooden box placed within the same marble casket within which the body had been found on May 4 of the year of salvation 1455. After this the wood-

en box was removed from the earlier marble casket and placed in another one above the altar in a central position on the wall, in the year of salvation 1566. Finally, after an authentication by the most eminent cardinal of the Holy Roman Church, Antonio Maria Erba Odescalchi, vicar of Rome, and after it was sealed within a more valuable container, it was deposited beneath the recently constructed altar, in the third year of the pontificate of Clement XIII, on August 1 of the year of redemption 1760.

Notwithstanding this testimony, questions remain. Since Father Casamassa's 1947 discovery of a fragment from a tomb—showing a few words from the inscription by Auchenius Bassus, prefect of Rome—some scholars have questioned the authenticity of the sepulcher located in the Church of St. Augustine, and therefore the relics themselves.

The faithful who come from every part of the world to Ostia to venerate St. Monica are still told that her tomb is located in the Church of St. Augustine. But if a fragment of the saint's sepulcher was still lying beneath the Church of Santa Aurea, whose was the sepulcher that was transferred during the reign of Martin V? One hypothetical solution seems most probable. The commission appointed by Pope Martin V was not required to conduct an exhaustive authentication in the task assigned to it. Perhaps St. Monica's casket had already been destroyed, leaving behind only fragments. In their haste to discover which of the different sepulchers was hers, the commissioners may have had to resort to taking one of the others in place of the real one. The last authentication of the contents was made in 1760, using the limited instruments of the time, under the supervision of Cardinal Vicar Antonio Odescalchi. Based upon those findings, the bones within the casket seem to be those of a young girl, which means they could not be St.

Monica's, since she died at the age of fifty-six. The remains are most likely those of a saint, possibly even a martyr, who lived before Monica, given that she had been laid to rest in the sacred place where a succession of worship sites had been built until the construction of the present basilica. As we have seen, the sepulchers of other saints were also discovered there.

And what of St. Monica's remains? They must still lie beneath the Basilica of Santa Aurea, but dispersed throughout the ground, since what was found was not an entire casket but only a fragment, which was proven authentic. No matter how accurate this reconstruction of events may be, devotion certainly does not depend upon relics; it expresses itself above all through prayer and the effort in imitation.

The devotion to St. Monica has steadily increased among Christians. Worthy of mention are the associations of "Christian mothers" that have arisen under St. Monica's protection and that aim to imitate her example.

As for her liturgical feast, the Roman Martyrology commemorates only the transfer of her relics, on April 9. In the new liturgical calendar prepared after the Second Vatican Council, no particular commemoration was retained for May 4, the date of the transfer of Monica's body to the casket in 1566. An obligatory memorial commemorating Monica was established for all the dioceses of the world, to be celebrated on August 27, the day before the feast of St. Augustine, who died in Hippo on August 28, 430.

In this way, St. Monica was taken from the sphere of private devotion and proposed as a model for the entire People of God. The proximity of the celebrations in honor of St. Monica and St. Augustine unites in the memory of the faithful and in the Church's solemn devotion these two lives, which were so closely united on earth.

CHAPTER XVI

Monica's Relevance for Families Today

The Church's purpose in canonization is not simply to reassure us that certain members are in God's glory and thus able to intercede for us. The beatification and canonization of saints provides us models to imitate. Even the souls of the deceased being purified after death are holy, because they participate in the divine life and enjoy God's friendship while interceding on our behalf. Through canonization, the Church selects from its "family album"—which embraces all of history—outstanding figures who have practiced virtue "to a heroic degree." The saints manifest God's victory and are examples for all of us to follow, both when making major life decisions and in our everyday situations.

The collective Christian imagination tends to think of sanctity in connection with those states of life characterized by special consecration to God. Marriage and life in the secular world, with its unique challenges, seems to preclude the possibility of exercising virtue heroically and thus providing an example for others. Apart from the martyrs—who were the only ones to receive special devotion during the first centuries of Christianity—the litanies of the saints single out the various categories of bishops, monks, and virgins. Sometimes they also mention widows. After the era of the martyrs, occasional exceptions were made for kings or queens, but even they adopted some form of vowed consecration to God after the death of their spouses. These persons were not really being proposed as models of holiness in marriage and society, but they were held up because of their martyrdom or penance.

Christian people may admire these illustrious individuals—and certainly they should—but such figures can seem removed from the everyday experience of most Christians. Because of this, it may be difficult to imitate these saints and follow their witness of faith concretely in daily life.

Closer to our own day, the Church, especially through the tireless work of John Paul II, has tried to bridge the gap that existed between a certain traditional type of sanctity and the faithful. Almost every Sunday in St. Peter's Square, and on almost every apostolic voyage, the pope elevated to the honor of the altar one or more saints or blesseds. No other pope in the history of the Church has canonized such a large number of exemplary Christian figures. It would not be far from the truth to say that John Paul II proclaimed more saints and blesseds than all the popes of the last two centuries, following the rigorous practices established by Urban VIII for causes of beatification and canonization.[79]

By doing this, John Paul II meant to show the Church and the world that the Holy Spirit produces fruits of sanctity in abundance and in many forms. Sanctity shines forth in every age, in every place, and in every vocation as proof of the supernatural character of the Church and the possibility of exercising heroic virtue in every situation and walk of life. Of the many recent canonizations, those that have elicited the most interest and been welcomed with the greatest gratitude by people all over the world are those of persons who have practiced a lay profession and lived the vocation of marriage and family. Particularly noteworthy figures include the obstetrician Giuseppe Moscati, wife and mother Gianna Beretta Molla, and the married couple Luigi and Maria Beltrame Quattrocchi, who were beatified together on November 25, 2001.

Ordinary people need figures they can identify with and with whom they can talk over their everyday problems, facing them with a Christian perspective and resolving them in the light of faith. One form of "modern" holiness can be seen in the family and in the lay vocation. In this sense, one may speak of St. Monica's relevance; although she lived almost seventeen centuries ago, she seems closer to us because she shared in the same difficulties and problems we experience today—especially family problems.

Today's families need models. This is a time of crisis for the family, with many types of behavior being adopted that are not inspired by Gospel values but instead are hedonistic, materialistic, and egoistic: conditional marriages, common-law unions, gay marriage, the exploitation and use of children as objects to be determined according to one's needs or preferences. In the face of this reality, what stance should Christians take? A reaction characterized solely by scathing criticism is not only tiresome but also ineffective. Christians fulfill the same role in the world as does the soul in the body. Rather than engage in useless complaining or exaggerate scenarios to catastrophic proportions, we must make a positive example of our own lives. The testimony of a family living in the joy that comes from love, reciprocal self-giving, and faithfulness proclaims the truth more effectively than a thousand speeches, which evaporate amid the countless words and messages bombarding us every day.

The answer to the many problems that afflict families certainly cannot be found in much of what we hear and read about each day: examples of celebrities who jump from one marriage to another as if it were a game; stories of adultery and love affairs without any moral reference; family squabbles that degenerate into violence; accounts of children without affection or guidance who plunge into drug addiction or other destructive patterns of behavior. One senses the need for something different, someone to speak a word of confidence and hope—a word not spoken verbally but with one's whole life. "Modern man," said Paul VI, "listens more willingly to witnesses than to teachers."[80]

The story of Monica's life is more relevant today than ever, because it is close to the problems we face in our own time. She had to come to terms with an adulterous, quarrelsome, and unbelieving husband. Despite her best efforts, she raised a son who ignored all moral norms and engaged in the most bizarre experiences, joining various religious sects. Although her methods of dealing with situations as a wife and mother in antiquity often vary from the kinds of solutions available to us today, Monica is still a witness for our time, not because she had a perfect family but because she did not run away from her responsibilities. She did not shut herself up in the ivory tower of her faith and religiosity, dismissing or ignoring the practical concerns of life. Neither did she lose or compromise her Christian identity, even though she threw herself entirely into the ambiguous situations of her family. She was like light, which remains pure even as it penetrates the darkness, and like salt, which does not become insipid by distributing itself through food. In the end, this is the Christian's mission, as Jesus lays it out in the Gospel (cf. Mt 5:13–16). Monica is a shining example for families today, bringing them courage and hope by guaranteeing that with the grace of God, good will, and perseverance, any difficulty can be overcome in building a true Christian family founded upon the values of the Gospel.

From the beginning of her marriage until the year before Patricius's death, Monica had to deal with a husband who did not believe in God. The difficulties of their life together, serious enough on account of Patricius's peculiar character, were aggravated by the fact that they did not share the same faith and therefore did not have the same vision of the world and meaning of life. This situation is by no means uncommon in our multiethnic, multicultural, and multireligious society.

The Christian who for various reasons has entered a mixed marriage with a person of another faith or with an agnostic or indifferent person should therefore not lose hope in the possibility of a married life characterized by a sharing of everything important and dear to the heart of a believer. After all, Monica used respect, patience, and especially the example of the happiness and interior strength that came from her faith to finally persuade Patricius to consider the real meaning of life and take the great step of conversion and baptism. Today, it is also possible to share married life with a person of a different faith and outlook without losing one's own identity, and while continuing to nourish oneself with the Word of God and the sacraments, giving a daily witness of serenity and joy to one's spouse and entire family.

Monica loved her husband tenderly, in spite of his many serious faults. Her secret was that she knew how to see and appreciate his good qualities and she knew how to bring out the best in him. This attitude was not something she took for granted but was the result of vigilance and daily effort. There must have been many occasions in which she had to strive to contain her natural resentment in the face of Patricius's unjustified tantrums and, even more seriously, his matrimonial infidelity. She armed herself with great patience and foresight just to keep her family life from becoming a living hell. In the end she triumphed, as St. Paul says, not being overcome by evil but overcoming evil with good (cf. Rom 12:21). She understood that repaying an offense with an offense was not a demonstration of strength but of weakness. Embracing the cross of Christ, she responded to the wrongs she received with forgiveness, which is the manifestation of love.

Forgiving does not mean approving of the wrong committed; rather, it means acting as Jesus did with the servant of the high priest who had struck him unjustly during his passion (cf. Jn 18:22–23). It means pointing out the wrong with patience and kindness at the appropriate time, so that the person who committed the action may become aware of the fault, correct it, and repair the wrong done. Authentic forgiveness comes from love; love means desiring the good of the other; and desiring the good of the other does not mean letting that person continue to inflict harm, but instead praying for and helping him or her to change.

St. Monica gives an example of holiness in marriage to those who are struggling with daily relationship difficulties with their spouse. A marital relationship can become a source of bitterness and suffering if it is lived in the name of egoism and self-seeking. If, instead, it is lived according to the plan of God, it can become a source of support, comfort, and joy. It must be sustained by real love, which entails self-giving, and by attentiveness and concern for the happiness of the other, which ends in one's own full realization and satisfaction.

Monica is also a model for families today. Children complete a family as the fruit of the reciprocal love of husband and wife. With the attitude that should set the Christian apart, Monica saw her children as gifts of God and not as her own possessions. She placed herself at their service, observing the natural inclinations of each one in order to discover the plan God had for them and help them accomplish their tasks in life in the best way possible. Each child, in fact, is an absolutely unique and unrepeatable person, who must be loved, nurtured, and accorded every opportunity for growth.

Unlike Patricius, Monica did not put her own plans or desires before those of God. Instead she put herself at the disposal of God's plan of salvation, helping each of her children—through her advice, encouragement, and above all her prayers—to follow the path of truth and goodness. Thus each of her children made good use of the talents he or she had received from the Lord, and each accomplished the plan of God: Perpetua by becoming a holy and wise abbess in her monastery, Navigius by forming a serene and exemplary Christian family, and Augustine by becoming a great source of enlightenment for the Church and the world, both during his time and for ages to come.

It is natural for a mother to give particular care to the child who needs her most, without in any way neglecting the others. So also Monica, seeing that Perpetua and Navigius were more well-grounded and needed less immediate care, concentrated her attention and efforts on Augustine. Although he excelled in intellectual gifts, his unruly and disordered life put him in sore need of Monica's guidance and prayers.

Many mothers today experience anxiety and deep concern for difficult or rebellious children. Such women may fight with all their strength, but sometimes they fall into depression and even despair because their efforts apparently come to nothing. St. Monica was untiringly tenacious in accompanying Augustine throughout his troubles and restless searching, which led him to embrace heresy and an immoral lifestyle.

St. Monica may have wept for her son, but she never conceded defeat. She prayed to the Lord. She summoned all her resources of mind and heart, adopting an attitude of extreme firmness or of reassurance and tenderness, depending on what the situation required. She asked for assistance from those who were able to provide it. On behalf of her son, she appealed to the most capable and respected persons, including Madaura's bishop, Agrippinus, and Ambrose, bishop of Milan. Despite the fact that she was an aging widow, she followed after Augustine —with no concern for her own discomfort—on a journey full of difficulties and dangers that brought her from Africa to Rome, and then to Milan.

Prayer, trust in God, and practical effort won for her victory in a battle that was certainly beyond her strength but one in which she continued with the inexhaustible energy that comes from the Lord. Her struggle, sufferings, and tears were rewarded beyond her wildest dreams, to the point that she was able to surrender her earthly life with these words:

> One thing only there was for which I desired to linger awhile in this life: to see you a Catholic Christian before I died. And this my God has granted to me more lavishly than I could have hoped, letting me see you even spurning earthly happiness to be his servant. What now keeps me here?[81]

St. Monica's example can comfort women living in similar situations. Although particular circumstances may vary, an essential similarity exists in the concerns these situations generate and the difficulties necessary in overcoming them. Considering how Monica reacted, and especially how she received the best conclusion she could have hoped for, could help one to ward off discouragement and could instill trust in those who find themselves involved in equally challenging circumstances.

Precisely because of her experience of the problems families often face today, because of her relevance and her profound humanity, perhaps one day the Church will proclaim her not only the patron of Christian mothers but of Christian families. Monica provides a model of behavior that has nothing miraculous or superhuman about it, only simplicity and daily effort. This is her great secret and value for families today.

Notes

1. This name is probably derived from the Punic name "Monna" or from the Latin "monna," meaning "mother" or "wife" as the word might be pronounced by children (cf. C. Egger, *Lexicon nominum virorum et mulierum,* second edition. Rome: Studium, 1963, pp. 170–171).

2. Monica was fifty-six years old when she died in 387, so she was born in 331 or 332 at the latest. Cf. *Confessions* IX, 11, 28.

3. *On the War with the Vandals* II.x.20.

4. The so-called "martyrs of Madaura," once believed to have come before the Scillitan martyrs, probably constitute an historical falsehood: they were fanatics of the Donatist sect, who are better known by the name of "Circumcellions." Cf. J. Baxter, *The martyrs of Madaura A.D. 180,* in the "Journal of Theological Studies," XXIV, 1924, pp. 21–37.

5. Tertullian, *Apologeticum,* 37. From the Rev. Alexander Roberts, D.D. and James Donaldson, LL.D., eds. *The Ante-Nicene Fathers: Translations of the Writings of the Fathers Down to A.D. 325. Volume III: Latin Christianity: Its Founder, Tertullian* (Wm. B. Eerdmans Publishing Company: Grand Rapids, MI, 1978).

6. Cf. *Letters* [of Cyprian] LXXI, 4; LXXIII, 3.

7. *Confessions* IX, 8, 17. All quotations from Augustine's Confessions excerpted from *The Confessions,* translated by Maria Boulding (Hyde Park, NY: New City Press, 1997).

8. *Confessions* IX, 8, 18.

9. John Chrysostom, *On the Priesthood* III, 17.

10. *Letter under the name of Augustine, to his sister, [detailing] the life and virtues of Saint Monica,* VII–VIII.

11. *Confessions* IX, 11, 28.

12. Tertullian, "To His Wife" II, 3–4. From the Rev. Alexander Roberts, D.D. and James Donaldson, LL.D., eds. *The Ante-Nicene Fathers: Translations of the Writings of the Fathers Down to A.D. 325. Volume IV: Tertullian, Part Fourth* (Grand Rapids, MI: Wm. B. Eerdmans Publishing Company, 1979).

13. *Life of Augustine* 1 ([pl] 32, 35).

14. *Confessions* IX, 9, 19.

15. Ibid., 9, 21.

16. Cf. *On the Happy Life* I:6 (*Idibus Novembris mihi natalis dies erat*).

17. Apart from Books VIII and IX of the *Confessions*, cf. *Letters* 211, 4.

18. *Life of Augustine*, 26, 1.

19. *Confessions* V, 9, 17.

20. Ibid., V, 9, 16.

21. *Confessions* IX, 9, 22.

22. Tertullian, *On Baptism* 18.

23. Cyprian, *Letter to Fidus* 2, 1.

24. *Confessions* I, 11, 17.

25. *Confessions* III, 4, 8.

26. *Confessions* VI, 5, 7–8.

27. Ibid., 16, 26.

28. *Against the [Academics]* II.ii.5. From Johannes Quasten, S.T.D. and Joseph C. Pulmpe, Ph.D., eds. *Ancient Christian Writers: The Works of the Fathers in Translation. St. Augustine: Against the Academics,* John J. O'Meara, translator and annotator (Westminster, MD: The Newman Press, 1950).

29. *Confessions* I, 11, 17.

30. Ibid., 11, 18.

31. Cf. H.I. Marrou, *Histoire de l'éducation dans l'antiquité* (Paris: Edition du Seuil, 1965); A. Quacquarelli, *Scuola e cultura dei primi secoli cristiani* (Brescia: La Scuola, 1974, pp. 35–39).

32. *Confessions* I, 9, 14.

33. *Confessions* II, 3, 7.

34. Ibid., 3, 8.

35. *Confessions* III, 11, 19.

36. Ibid., 11, 20.

37. Ibid., 12, 21. G. Papini is of the opinion that the bishop should be identified with Antigonus of Madaura (see *Sant'Agostino,* Florence: Vallecchi, 1929, pp. 73–74).

38. *Confessions* V, 8, 15.

39. Ibid., 9, 16–17.

40. *Confessions* VI, 1, 1.

41. Council of Nicea (A.D. 325), canon 2; Council of Sardica (A.D. 343), canon 10.

42. *Confessions* VI, 2, 2.

43. *Letters of Augustine,* 36, 14–32. From Philip Schaff, D.D., LL.D., ed. *A Select Library of the Nicene and Post-Nicene Fathers of the Christian Church. Volume I: The Confessions and Letters of St. Augustine, With a Sketch of His Life and Work* (Grand Rapids, MI: Wm. B. Eerdmans Publishing Company, 1974).

44. For this entire chapter, cf. A. Paredi, *Saint Ambrose: His Life and Times* (Notre Dame, IN: University of Notre Dame Press, 1964).

45. *Confessions* VI, 6, 9.

46. Ibid., 15, 25.

47. Ibid., 15, 25.

48. *Confessions* VIII, 8, 19.

49. Ibid., 12, 28–30.

50. *On Order* II.xx.52.

51. *On the Gift of Perseverance* XX, 53.

52. The identification of "Cassiciacum" with Cassago in Brianza seems the most feasible, and it also seems that its identification with Casciago in Varese should be definitively dismissed. Moreover, the proper pronunciation would be "Cassiaco," even though tradition—from the monks of the order of St. Mauro onward—reads this as "Cassiciaco." In this regard, cf. the critical edition of the *Confessions* produced by A. C. Vega (Madrid: BAC, 1963, IX.xi.370). I have followed this volume especially for its precise and exhaustive notes, even though the work arrives at some of its conclusions too quickly, as if they could be taken for granted.

53. *On Order* I.viii.22–23.

54. *On the Happy Life* II:8. All quotations from *On the Happy Life* excerpted from Ludwig Schopp, ed. *The Fathers of the Church: A New Translation. Writings of Saint Augustine: Volume I* (New York: Cima Publishing Co., Inc., 1948).

55. *On the Happy Life* II:8.

56. Ibid., II:9.

57. Ibid., II:10.

58. Ibid., III:21.

59. Ibid., IV:27.

60. Ibid., IV:27.

61. Ibid., IV:35.

62. *On Order* II.I.1. On the overall question of Monica's philosophical attitude, cf. the interesting introduction to the dialogues written by V. Capanaga, in *Obras de San Augustin,* vol. I (Madrid: BAC 10, 1969, 4th edition, pp. 397–434).

63. Manlius Theodorus was a prominent personage, a Christian, and one of Augustine's close friends. He served as prefect of Libya, prefect of Macedonia, the emperor's chief distributor of alms, prefect of Gaul in 380,

and consul in 399. Augustine met him in 386, and the two sought truth together through Platonic philosophy. Augustine dedicated his dialogue *On the Happy Life* to Theodorus.

64. *On Order* I.xi.31–33.

65. Ibid., II.viii.22–23.

66. How the rites of Christian initiation during the Easter vigil were carried out in Milan at the end of the fourth century can be seen in Ambrose's work *On the Mysteries.*

67. *Confessions* IX, 6, 14.

68. Ibid., IX, 10, 23–25.

69. Ibid., IX, 10, 26.

70. Ibid., IX, 11, 27.

71. Ibid., IX, 11, 28.

72. Ibid., IX, 11, 28; 7, 29–33; 13, 34–37.

73. Augustine would have turned thirty-four on November 13, so Monica's death must have occurred before that date, some time between May and November. Her death most likely took place during the summer, because voyages were undertaken during the temperate season.

74. *Confessions* IX, 12, 33.

75. Ibid., 13, 34–37.

76. *On the Care of the Dead* 16. From Philip Schaff, D.D., LL.D., ed. *A Select Library of the Nicene and Post-Nicene Fathers of the Christian Church. Volume III: St. Augustin: On the Holy Trinity, Doctrinal Treatises, Moral Treatises* (Grand Rapids, MI: Wm. B. Eerdmans Publishing Company, 1978).

77. Cf. N. Concetti, *Circa corporis Sanctae Monicae translationem* [On the transfer of the body of St. Monica], in "Analecta augustiniana," volume 5 (1913–1914), pp. 229–234; volume 6 (1915–1916), pp. 110–111.

78. A. Casamassa, *L'autore di un preteso discorso di Martino V* [The author of a speech attributed to Martin V], in *Miscellanea, Pio Paschini I* (Rome: Pontifical Lateran University, 1948, pp. 109–125); idem, *Ritrovamento di parte dell'elogio di S. Monica* [The rediscovery of part of the eulogy for St. Monica], in *Scritti patristici I* (ibid., 1995, pp. 215–218).

79. Constitution *Coelestis Jerusalem,* July 7, 1634.

80. *Evangelii nuntiandi,* December 8, 1975, no. 41. Cf. *Sermo habitus ad sodales "Consilii de Laicis,"* October 2, 1974.

81. *Confessions* IX, 10, 26.

Index of References

St. Monica within St. Augustine's Works
(as referenced within this text)

BOOKS & MEDIA

The Daughters of St. Paul operate book and media centers at the following addresses. Visit, call or write the one nearest you today, or find us on the World Wide Web, www.pauline.org

CALIFORNIA
3908 Sepulveda Blvd, Culver City, CA 90230   310-397-8676
2640 Broadway Street, Redwood City, CA 94063   650-369-4230
5945 Balboa Avenue, San Diego, CA 92111   858-565-9181

FLORIDA
145 S.W. 107th Avenue, Miami, FL 33174   305-559-6715

HAWAII
1143 Bishop Street, Honolulu, HI 96813   808-521-2731
Neighbor Islands call: 866-521-2731

ILLINOIS
172 North Michigan Avenue, Chicago, IL 60601   312-346-4228

LOUISIANA
4403 Veterans Memorial Blvd, Metairie, LA 70006   504-887-7631

MASSACHUSETTS
885 Providence Hwy, Dedham, MA 02026   781-326-5385

MISSOURI
9804 Watson Road, St. Louis, MO 63126   314-965-3512

NEW JERSEY
561 U.S. Route 1, Wick Plaza, Edison, NJ 08817   732-572-1200

NEW YORK
150 East 52nd Street, New York, NY 10022   212-754-1110

PENNSYLVANIA
9171-A Roosevelt Blvd, Philadelphia, PA 19114   215-676-9494

SOUTH CAROLINA
243 King Street, Charleston, SC 29401   843-577-0175

TENNESSEE
4811 Poplar Avenue, Memphis, TN 38117   901-761-2987

TEXAS
114 Main Plaza, San Antonio, TX 78205   210-224-8101

VIRGINIA
1025 King Street, Alexandria, VA 22314   703-549-3806

CANADA
3022 Dufferin Street, Toronto, ON M6B 3T5   416-781-9131

¡También somos su fuente para libros,
videos y música en español!